9-11 ON TRIAL

The World Trade Center

Collapse

BY

VICTOR THORN

Sisyphus

Press

9-11 On Trial:

The World Trade Center Collapse

by Victor Thorn

Progressive Press Edition

QUESTION THE OFFICIAL 9/11 CONSPIRACY THEORY

2006

SISYPHUS PRESS

P.O. Box 10495

State College, Pennsylvania 16805

Copyright 2005 by Victor Thorn

WING TV

www.wingtv.net

Second edition, June 2006

Published by **Progressive Press**

P.O. Box 126, Joshua Tree, CA 92252

www.ProgressivePress.com

Library of Congress Subject Classification:

September 11 Terrorist Attacks, 2001.

Terrorism—Government Policy—United States

ISBN-10: 0-930852-87-7.

ISBN-13: 978-0-930852-87-0.

LCCN applied for.

Printed in the United States of America

TABLE OF CONTENTS

8/27/07

ACKNOWLEDGEMENTS

I would like to extend my deepest appreciation to the following authors, researchers, and organizations whose work I have referenced during the course of *9-11 on Trial*: Eric Hufschmid, Jim Hoffman & Don Paul, Christopher Bollyn and everyone at the *American Free Press*, David Ray Griffin, Jerry Russell & Richard Stanley, Dave McGowan, Jim Marrs, J. McMichael, George Humphrey, Peter Meyer, Jeff King, Colin Bett, Ralph Omholt, Geronimo Jones, Abel Ashes, Fintan Dunne, Kevin Ryan from the Environmental Health Laboratories, Prof. Michel Chossudovsky and the Centre for Research on Globalization, the Vancouver Independent Media Organization, the L.A. Independent Media Organization, and the University of Sydney's Department of Civil Engineering. Without their fantastic insight into what actually happened on the morning of September 11, 2001, this book would not be possible. If you are interested in finding out more about 9-11, their books, articles, and videos are a perfect place to start. (For more information, please see the "References" section at the end of this book, or click onto the *9-11 on Trial* link at: http://www.wingtv.net.

Also, I would like to thank my WING TV co-host, Lisa Guliani, for her unending search for the truth, her amazing work ethic, and everything she brings to our daily television show. Her energy is what keeps me going each day. Secondly, a standing ovation to Mr. Peter Currenti for helping us with not only our website, but also for the amazing book covers he has created over the years. As I always say, I couldn't imagine doing a book without him. Thirdly, kudos to John Kaminski, whose work I have been privileged to publish (*The Day America Died, The Perfect Enemy*), and whose ear I've chewed off on many occasions talking about the 9-11 phenomenon.

We would also like to acknowledge the following 9-11 researchers (not already mentioned) who have appeared on WING TV during the past year: Phil Jayhan, Dave Von Kleist, Daniel Hopsicker, Russ Wittenberg, Tom Flocco, Michael Elliott, Kyle Hence, Nico Haupt, Anthony Hilder, Dylan Avery, Kee Dewdney, Stanley Hilton, Karl Schwarz, Jimmy Walter, John Leonard, Donn de Grand Pre, and Webster Tarpley. These individuals keep the 9-11 Truth Movement alive.

Last, but certainly not least, Lisa Guliani and I would like to thank the following individuals who have had us on their radio show, or reviewed, blurbed, did artwork for, distributed our books, or assisted with our website: Michael Collins Piper, Vyzygoth, Jack Blood, Meria Heller, Alex Merklinger, Rick Biesada, Keidi Awadu, Pastor Daniel Johns, Sherry Shriner, Michael Corbin, Gordon Thomas, John Tiffany, Paul Walker, Joyce Metzger, Rick Stanley, Lieutenant Colonel Daniel Marvin, Jeffrey Bennett, Vince Ryan, Clay Douglas, Georgeann Hughes, Bank Index, Duncan Long, Louis Turner, Gogue, Ellen Kimball, Ann Cronin of First Amendment Books, Andy Carey, Kendall H., Adventures Unlimited, *The Daily Collegian*, Carol Brouillet, Adam Schlosser, Thomas Fortenberry, The Midwest Book Review, *Clamor* magazine, and *Voices of Central Pennsylvania*.

NOTES ON THE TEXT

9-11 on Trial was comprised from research that has already been established in the form of books, articles, and videotapes. These sources can be found in the "References" section near the end of this book. As its title implies, I am relaying this information in transcript form as if it took place in any actual courtroom across America. Hopefully that day will soon arrive so that the guilty parties can be held accountable for their atrocious actions. To present this material in the most accurate way possible, I have used the exact quotes as they appeared in their original form. The only minor alterations occur when a change in tense or grammar was needed to preserve the dialogue's flow or to ensure ease of reading.

Also, a vast array of supplemental photographic evidence is available on the WING TV website under the link entitled *9-11 on Trial*. It is categorized according to witness chapters, and is an invaluable resource to more fully understand all of the discrepancies in the "official" version of events.

OPENING
STATEMENT

LADIES AND GENTLEMEN OF THE JURY, what if you discovered that it was impossible for the World Trade Center towers to collapse the way the government said they did, and that there was a zero-percent chance that their "official" version of events was true? How would this news affect your view of what happened that day, and particularly of your elected 'leaders' who supposedly have your best interests in mind?

Before answering, take a moment and return to the morning of September 11, 2001 when you first heard that the Twin Towers had been struck by jetliners. Do you remember people jumping hundreds of feet to their deaths, television screens repeatedly flashing the words TERROR ALERT, the screams, panic, flames, smoke, and ultimately the towers collapsing into their own footprint? Step back to that fateful day when you heard reports that New York City was ordering 10,000 body bags, when you saw pictures of rescue workers cradling dead babies in their arms, and the look of horror on people's faces as they fled down the panicked streets of Manhattan.

With these thoughts bouncing through your mind, let me ask you a question. Considering the trauma created by this horrendous event, do you think we as American citizens deserve to know the 100% absolute truth about what took place that day? Not just half-truths, misinformation, and obfuscation; but the truth, the whole truth, and nothing but the truth. This isn't asking too much, is it?

Think about it. On the morning of 9-11 we were attacked; we were betrayed, and nearly 3,000 of our fellow Americans were murdered in cold blood. Now, if there were even a one-percent chance that the government's "official" version of events was inaccurate or false, shouldn't we do everything humanly possible to discover what the truth really is? Furthermore, can't we even go so far as to say that it's our obligation to find out what actually happened that day? I mean, if the search for truth and justice in regard to 9-11 doesn't matter to us, what in God's name does?

In this light, our biggest dilemma remains: does the truth matter? This question is crucial, because during the course of this trial we will prove beyond a shadow of a doubt that the United States government's "official" version of events in regard to how the WTC towers collapsed is an absolute, undeniable lie. To do so, we will chip away at, erode, and ultimately destroy their cover story in a very methodical, chronological way. As we build to a crescendo, we'll reach a point where the preponderance of evidence is so overwhelming against the official version of events that you'll realize that the <u>truth</u> is even more horrifying than what we were led to believe happened on 9-11.

And what, you may wonder, is the truth? What actually *did* happen on the morning of 9-11? We will show that the Twin Towers did not collapse due to burning jet fuel which resulted from the impact of two jetliners crashing into them. Instead, the WTC towers, along with WTC 7, were deliberately destroyed in controlled demolitions that had been planned and prepared far in advance of 9-11.

Considering the trauma induced by 9-11, I realize that any deviation from the "official" story will be met with a great deal of resistance in certain circles (despite the many polls which state that Americans are very skeptical of this very same "official" story). Some will undoubtedly even say: why complicate matters with a "conspiracy theory"? But as you'll see, we absolutely will not utilize theories of any kind in the prosecution of this trial. And in all honesty, that would be very easy for us, for the government's story has more holes in it than a huge block of Swiss cheese.

But rather than rely on theory, we are going to do something that horrifies the federal government: we're going to show, using scientific proof, physics, mathematical formulas, the laws of nature, and expert testimony that it was <u>physically impossible</u> for the towers to fall in accordance with the "official" version of events. And by the time we conclude our presentation of evidence in this case, you too will not be able to deny this preponderance of evidence.

To close, let's return once again to a question I asked earlier: does the truth matter to us, especially in relation to 9-11 – an event that traumatized and impacted this nation more than any other in its history? If the truth does matter, then listen very carefully to what our upcoming witnesses have to say. As you do so, we guarantee that your eyes will be opened to something we've seen far too little of from our government – the truth.

WITNESS ONE
The "Official" Story

Ladies and gentlemen, to understand our frame of reference in this case, you must first become acquainted with precisely what we're standing in opposition against. Specifically, our first witness will now present to you what has become known as the "official version" of 9-11.

Question: What has come to represent the official version of 9-11?

Witness 1: Essentially, four sources comprise the official version of 9-11.

Question: What would these four sources be?

Witness 1: In terms of when they appeared, these sources would be:

1) A BBC article by Sheila Barter entitled *How the World Trade Center Fell* – September 13, 2001

2) Zdenek Bazant & Yong Zhou's article *Why Did the World Trade Center Collapse? – Simple Analysis –* September 13, 2001, *Journal of Engineering Mechanics*

3) PBS Nova Special – *Why the Towers Fell –* produced and directed by Garfield Kennedy and Larry Klein – April 30, 2002

4) FEMA's *World Trade Center Building Performance Study –* May, 2002

Question: Could you briefly summarize the official version of events in regard to the World Trade Center's collapse?

Witness 1: "Two Boeing jetliners were deliberately crashed into the twin towers, causing raging fires within, which melted the steel support structures, thereby causing the buildings to collapse completely." (23)

Question: Since you mentioned fire, let's start there. What role did burning jet fuel play in the collapse of the towers?

Witness 1: According to Geronimo Jones, who referenced the BBC article, "The collapse of the towers was a direct result of the plane crashes, whose fires blazing hot from the jet fuel, created temperatures in excess of 800 degrees Celsius (1472 degrees F) and caused the steel supports to melt, leading to the towers' collapse." (5)

Question: What else did the BBC report have to say on this matter?

Witness 1: They quoted structural engineer Chris Wise, who said, "It was the fire that killed the buildings. There is nothing on earth that could survive those temperatures with that amount of fuel burning. The columns would have melted, the floors would have melted, and eventually they would have collapsed on top of one another." (19)

Question: FEMA – the Federal Emergency Management Agency – also weighed in on this matter, didn't they?

Witness 1: Yes, they said that "The structural damage sustained by each tower from the impact, combined with the ensuing fires, resulted in the total collapse of each building." (37)

Question: So, once again fire appears to be the main culprit?

Witness 1: Yes, FEMA stated, "As each aircraft impacted a building, jet fuel on board ignited. Part of this fuel immediately burned off in large fireballs that erupted at the impact floors. Remaining fuel flowed across the floors and down elevator and utility shafts, igniting intense fires throughout upper portions of the buildings. As these fires spread, they further weakened the steel-framed structures, eventually leading to total collapse." (37)

Question: Did other sources confirm the story that fires led to the World Trade Center's collapse?

Witness 1: Yes, on September 24, 2001, CNN reported, "The collapse, when it came, was caused by fire. The fire was very, very intense and burned for a long time. The fire weakened that portion of the structure which remained after the impact. It was weakened by fire to the point where it could no longer sustain the load." (12)

Question: Any other sources?

Witness 1: *Civil Engineering Magazine* reported, "The fires burned at such a high temperature that a stream of molten metal began to pour over the side of the tower. The heat output from these fires will later be estimated to have been comparable to that produced by a large nuclear generating station." (11)

Question: Were there any other contributing factors to the towers' collapse?

Witness 1: Yes. "The loss of strength and stiffness of the material resulting from the fire, combined with the initial impact damage, would have caused the failure of the truss system supporting the floor." (8)

Question: What role did the trusses play?

Witness 1: "According to the WTC report, 1½ inch, 22-gauge non-composite steel deck trusses were supported at the inner core on seats off a girder which ran continuously past and was supported by the core columns. The only thing securing trusses to the inner core were 5/8" bolts." (13)

Question: Could you elaborate further?

Witness 1: In the official account, "The floor-plate attachments are supposed to have let go; causing the accelerating cement "pancake" mass. According to this theory, only the first floor above the fire initially collapsed, causing the floors below to progressively collapse, one-floor-at-a-time." (16) In addition, according to the Massachusetts

Institute of Technology (MIT), "The single-bolt connections in the framework of the World Trade Center popped and fell apart during the September 11 terrorist attacks, causing the floors to collapse on top of each other.   This analysis concludes that the bolts did not properly secure the towers' steel floor trusses." (13)

Question: Were there any other possibilities for this collapse?

Witness 1: Bazant and Zhou came up with a 'column failure' theory two days after the attacks which is now referred to as the "wet noodle" theory. (19)

Question: What precisely does this "wet noodle" theory entail?

Witness 1: "Heat from the fire supposedly caused the columns not to melt, but to lose most of their strength by softening because steel starts to soften long before it melts at high temperatures." (19)

Question: How were the trusses you referred to earlier attached to the World Trade Center itself?

Witness 1: "The official story has it that the towers collapsed because (a) the only connection between the outer perimeter wall and the central core were flimsy lightweight trusses. (b) The plane impact weakened these trusses and the heat of the fires caused them to buckle until (c) the trusses at the impact floors gave way and (d) the floors above lost their support and fell upon the lower floors causing all floors to pancake." (23)

Question: With this information in mind, please summarize the government's official version of events.

Witness 1: "Heat from the fires weakened or softened the trusses that supported the floors. Either from sagging or thermal expansion of the trusses, the attachments of the outer end of the trusses to the outer steel framework of the buildings were broken. This would presumably happen to the floor or floors above the impact sites, where the fires would

8/27/07

Tu
8/28/07

have burned hottest. The loss of these attachments is then said to have caused entire floors or sections of floors to fall, leading to a chain-reaction collapse." (22)

Question: One last question: in FEMA's *World Trade Center Building Performance Study*, it is written: "With the information and time available, the sequence of events leading to the collapse of each tower could not be definitively determined." (37) Why did the investigators ultimately reach this non-definitive conclusion?

Witness 1: "There is so little information because the rubble was <u>destroyed</u> and our investigation was 'hampered'." (41)

WITNESS TWO
Evidence Tampering

Ladies and gentlemen of the jury, whenever a crime is committed, the accused always say, "Prove it – show us the evidence." And since we're here with you today, it seems very clear that this is precisely what we'd like to do. In fact, we'd <u>love</u> to show you evidence from the World Trade Center towers. But we can't do that. Why? Because the government – with lightning speed – immediately sent haulers into Ground Zero to cart away all the evidence; the evidence being, of course, the steel girders from which the towers were constructed.

Now ask yourselves a question: what is the first thing that is supposed to happen to evidence at a crime scene? The answer is that it's supposed to be sealed off and not tampered with until it can be officially inspected. This is common sense 101, and you don't have to watch Columbo or Perry Mason to know that. Yet what did the government do at this crime scene? They disregarded every protocol and procedural rule and got rid of the evidence. Why?

Question: Would you consider the terror attacks of 9-11 a crime?

Witness 2: I would.

Question: And would the World Trade Center rubble be considered evidence at a crime scene?

Witness 2: It would.

Question: With this rudimentary scenario in mind, what was given highest priority after 9-11: the inspection of rubble at the Ground Zero crime scene, or the removal of this evidence?

Witness 2: "Disposal of rubble was given first priority." (41)

Question: Does this decision seem peculiar to you?

Witness 2: Bill Manning, editor of a 125-year-old firefighting magazine called *Fire Engineering,* said in the January, 2002 edition: "Except for the marginal benefit obtained from a three-day visual walk-through of evidence sites conducted by the ASCE (American Society of Civil Engineers) investigation committee members – described by a close source as a 'tourist trip' – no one's checking the evidence for anything. The destruction and removal of evidence must stop immediately." (43)

Question: Did others mentioned in this article have any objections to this practice?

Witness 2: In the same issue of this magazine, "A number of fire officials, including a retired deputy chief from New York's fire department, called on FEMA to immediately impanel a World Trade Center Disaster Review panel to coordinate a complete review of all aspects of the World Trade Center incident." (43)

Question: What were these individuals so upset about?

Witness 2: "These fire officials noted that the WTC disaster was the largest loss of firefighters ever at one incident; the second largest loss of life on American soil; the first total collapse of a high-rise during a fire in United States history, and the largest structural collapse in recorded history. Now, with that understanding, you would think we would have had the largest fire investigation in world history. But you would be wrong. Instead, we have a series of unconnected and uncoordinated superficial inquiries. We are literally treating the steel removed from the site like garbage, not like crucial fire scene evidence." (43) (44)

Question: Before we delve into what was specifically hauled away from this crime scene, were limits placed on those investigators seeking access to the crippled towers?

Witness 2: "Investigators were barred from Ground Zero. People were threatened with arrest for merely taking photographs." (19) Plus, "The people who were destroying the rubble were quickly passed through the checkpoints, while the investigators were often delayed for hours." (41) Lastly, "On January 25, 2002 Vice President Cheney called Senator Daschle on the phone and asked him to limit the scope and the overall review of what happened on 9-11." (41)

Question: How much evidence was removed from this site?

Witness 2: According to the *New York Daily News*, "185,101 tons of structural steel had been hauled away from Ground Zero." (34)

Question: Was all of this evidence inspected?

Witness 2: According to the same source, "About 80% of the steel was scrapped without being examined." (34)

Question: How would you describe this removal process?

Witness 2: "The evidence was being destroyed as rapidly as possible." (19)

Question: What we're talking about here is crucial evidence from a crime scene?

Witness 2: Yes. "The evidence is the structural steel – that's what holds the buildings up; that's what you would look at to try to understand what caused these steel buildings to collapse." (19)

Question: Who was in charge of removing this steel?

Witness 2: A company called Controlled Demolition, Inc.

Question: And when did this process begin?

Witness 2: "The city accepted a plan by Controlled Demolition to recycle the steel a mere eleven days after the attacks." (19)

Question: Recycle it in eleven days?

Witness 2: Yes, Controlled Demolition, Inc. "was able to come up with a detailed plan within eleven days of the collapse of the Twin Towers." (20)

Question: Were there any special precautions taken when this evidence was being removed?

Witness 2: A couple. First, "new infrastructure in the form of docks were created to expedite the removal." (19) Plus, "on November 26, 2001, the city initiated the use of an in-vehicle GPS tracking system to monitor locations of trucks hired to haul the debris to Fresh Kills, the official dump site on Staten Island." (34)

Question: Was this standard procedure for disposing of scrap?

Witness 2: No. "In the weeks before launching the GPS system, the city relied on a paper-based system for tracking traffic and loading data." (34)

Question: Until they got the GPS system to guard this scrap, how was it transported to the dump?'

Witness 2: "Police and several other agencies teamed-up to monitor the trucks on their routes between Ground Zero through 20 to 30 miles of tunnels, bridges and highways to the dump on Staten Island." (34)

Question: Once all this steel reached the scrap yard, what happened next?

Witness 2: "Much of the structural steel from the World Trade Center was sold to Alan D. Ratner of Metal Management of Newark, New Jersey; and the New York-based company Hugo Neu Schnitzer East." (5)

Question: And then what?

Witness 2: "Ratner quickly sold the WTC steel to overseas companies, reportedly selling more than 50,000 tons of steel to a Shanghai steel company known as Baosteel for $120 per ton." (5) Also, the steel "was recycled as per the city's decision to swiftly send the wreckage to salvage yards in New Jersey" (34) or "whisked onto ships bound for blast furnaces in India and China." (19)

Question: Yet this "scrap" required GPS tracking units and police escorts. Now, moving ahead, who was given the responsibility of investigating the World Trade Center wreckage?

Witness 2: FEMA.

Question: Are they an investigative agency?

Witness 2: "FEMA was entrusted with the responsibility of investigating the collapses even though it's not an investigative agency." (19)

Question: Was an independent investigation ever sanctioned by the government?

Witness 2: "No independent investigation was funded." (36)

Question: Now, we must remember that WTC 1, WTC 2, and WTC 7 were the largest structural failures in American history. How did FEMA proceed?

Witness 2: "FEMA assembled a group of volunteer investigators; the Building Performance Assessment Team (BPAT), and gave them a budget of $600,000." (36)

Question: What is the budget for Homeland Security projected to be in 2005?

Witness 2: The Department of Homeland Security reports that it will be $40.2 billion.

Question: So this would be about 1/1000th of 1% of the current Homeland Security budget?

Witness 2: Correct.

Question: Continuing on, were the BPAT investigators allowed access to Ground Zero?

Witness 2: No. "They were only allowed to examine a few large pieces of steel that made it to Fresh Kills landfill." (36)

Question: And how long did their investigation last?

Witness 2: "Their analysis was only from October 7-12." (36)

Not according to FEMA Report

Question: During these five days of study, did FEMA investigate the possible use of explosives?

Witness 2: "While steel is often tested for evidence of explosions, despite numerous eyewitness reports of explosions in the towers, the engineers involved in the FEMA-sponsored building assessment did no such tests." (5)

Question: Who was in charge of this FEMA project?

Witness 2: "Dr. W. Gene Corley – who investigated for the government the cause of the fire at the Branch Davidian compound in Waco and the Oklahoma City bombing – headed the FEMA-sponsored engineering assessment of the WTC collapse." (5)

Question: Did Corley say why no specific explosives tests were performed?

Witness 2: Yes. "Corley told AFP (*American Free Press*) that while some tests had been done on the 80 pieces of steel saved from the site, we did not know about tests that show if an explosion had affected the steel." (5)

Question: Did he give a reason?

Witness 2: Yes, "I am not a metallurgist" he said. (5)

Question: Has there been any criticism directed at this FEMA investigation?

Witness 2: Yes, quite a bit.

Question: Could you give us a sampling of this criticism?

Witness 2: (a) Science Committee of the House of Representatives – March 6, 2002: "Their report concluded that the investigation was "hampered." One problem was that clean-up crews arrived the same day and immediately began disposing of the rubble. The result was: some of the critical pieces of steel were gone before the first investigator ever reached the site. When investigators finally arrived at the site they discovered they were subservient to the clean-up crews: the lack of authority of investigators to impound pieces of steel for examination before they were recycled led to the loss of important pieces of evidence." (41)

(b) <u>Congressman Sherwood Boehlert (R-NY)</u> – March 7, 2002 – Opening Statement for the World Trade Center Hearing: "I must say that the current investigation seems to be shrouded in excessive secrecy." (41)

(c) <u>David Ray Griffin</u> – *The New Pearl Harbor* – "After the collapse of the towers, the debris, including the steel, was quickly removed before there could be any significant investigation. *The New York Times* complained, saying: the decision to rapidly recycle the steel columns, beams and trusses from the WTC in the days immediately after 9/11 means definitive answers may never be known." (46)

(d) <u>New York Daily News</u> – *Firefighter Magazine Raps 9/11 Probe* – Joe Calderone – January 4, 2002: "Interviews with a handful of members of the team, which included some of the nation's most respected engineers, uncovered complaints that they had at various times been shackled with bureaucratic restrictions that prevented them from interviewing witnesses, examining the disaster site and requesting crucial information like recorded distress calls to the police and fire departments." (21)

(e) <u>Dr. Frederick W. Mowrer</u> – University of Maryland – Fire Engineering Department: "I find the speed with which important evidence has been removed and recycled has been appalling." (21)

Question: Were there any other criticisms of this investigation?

Witness 2: Yes, the most damning assessment came from Bill Manning, editor of the 125-year-old *Fire Engineering* magazine in the January, 2002 edition.

Question: What did he say?

Witness 2: He began by noting how different the removal of evidence was from the World Trade Center in comparison to other New York City fires: "Did they throw away the locked doors from the Triangle Shirtwaist Fire? Did they throw away the gas can used at the Happy Land Social Club fire? That's what they're doing at the World Trade Center. The destruction and removal of evidence must stop immediately." (21)

Question: Anything else?

Witness 2: He continued, "For more than three months, structural steel from the World Trade Center has been, and continues to be, cut up and sold for scrap. Crucial evidence that could answer many questions about high-rise building design practices and performances under fire conditions is on a slow boat to China, perhaps never to be seen again in America until you buy your next car." He continued, "*Fire Engineering* has good reason to believe that the 'official investigation' blessed by FEMA and run by the American Society of Civil Engineers (ASCE) is a half-baked farce that may already have been commandeered by political forces whose primary interest, to put it mildly, lie far afield of full disclosure." (43)

Question: Does this constitute the entirety of the criticism?

Witness 2: There is plenty more, but I'll refer you to this statement by Peter Meyer in his article, *The World Trade Center Demolition*: "The WTC debris was removed as fast as possible and no forensic examination of the debris was permitted. Almost all the 300,000 tons of steel from the Twin Towers was sold to New York scrap dealers and exported to places like China and Korea as quickly as it could be loaded onto ships, thereby removing the evidence." (46)

Question: Of the 300,000 tons of steel, how many pieces were examined by FEMA volunteers?

Witness 2: "[Gene] Corley told AFP that some tests had been done on the <u>80</u> pieces of steel saved from the site." (15)

Tu 8/28/07

WITNESS THREE
World Trade Center Design

To understand what impact the planes and fire had on the World Trade Center towers, we need to look very closely at how these buildings were constructed.

Question: How tall were the World Trade Center Towers?

Witness 3: "1,368 feet and 1,362 feet." (37)

Question: And how long was the base of each structure?

Witness 3: "207 feet." (37)

Question: So, to walk along the sidewalk of one side of one tower would be like walking 2/3 of a football field, and then the next side would be 2/3 of a football field, and the third side would be 2/3 of a football, and the final side would be 2/3 of a football field? (37)

Witness 3: Yes.

Question: And how much area was contained within each floor?

Witness 3: "Nearly an acre on each floor." (37)

Question: Most people would be very pleased to have a half-acre plot of land for their house. So, every floor of each 110 story building was nearly an acre in size?

Witness 3: This is true.

Question: Needless to say, these structures were enormous.

Witness 3: They were.

Question: Okay, in laymen's terms, how were these towers constructed?

Witness 3: The primary elements to each tower were enormous steel and concrete cores which "were designed to support the entire weight of the buildings several times over." (12)

Question: Were these central columns merely service cores that housed elevator and utility shafts?

Witness 3: No, "there were 47 steel box columns tied together at each floor by steel plates, similar to the 52-inch deep spandrel plates that tied the perimeter columns together." (12)

Question: To give us some perspective, how huge were these core columns?

Witness 3: "The largest of these core columns were 18" x 36", with steel walls 4" thick near the base." (12)

Question: And how were these towers connected to the ground they stood on?

Witness 3: "The foundations of the Twin Towers were 70 feet deep. At that level, 47 huge box columns, connected to the bedrock, supported the entire gravity load of the structures." (15)

Question: So they extended seven stories below the streets of Manhattan?

Witness 3: Correct.

Question: Again, how massive were these columns?

Witness 3: "The steel walls of these lower box columns were four inches thick." (15)

Question: And how were the towers held together?

Witness 3: "Each tower was supported by a lattice of 90,000 tons of steel strong enough to resist earthquakes and hurricane-force winds." (45)

Question: When we examine the government's official version of events, one gets the impression that these towers were somewhat flimsy in their construction. Is this true?

Witness 3: "The World Trade Center was made with some of the largest, strongest fire-retardant steel beams of any building in history." (9)

Question: Considering its obvious strength, how much was each floor designed to hold?

Witness 3: According to the PBS/NOVA companion website for their documentary, *How the Towers Fell*, "each floor was designed to hold 1,300 tons beyond its own weight." (2)

Question: Since a ton equals 2,000 pounds, that's 2,600,000 pounds beyond its own weight?

Witness 3: Correct.

Question: And what, once again, constituted its strength?

Witness 3: "The core was built of sheer concrete reinforced by 44 beams of construction grade steel which took up the majority of the tower's footprint." (5)

Question: As we have seen from the government's official version of events, they purport that the towers collapsed after one floor fell down on another, creating a pancake affect. Is this theory consistent with the towers' design?

Witness 3: "In the World Trade Center towers, concrete was only a <u>flooring</u> material. It was <u>not</u> holding the building together. Rather, the building was a three-dimensional network of steel." (41)

Question: So, unlike bridges or other <u>concrete</u> structures, the World Trade Center towers were truly <u>steel</u> buildings?

Witness 3: Yes. "Each floor was a network of steel beams, covered by a corrugated steel deck, which in turn was filled with concrete." (41)

Question: Describe this arrangement.

Witness 3: "The concrete was four inches thick, which gave it substantial strength, but to describe the floors as being "slabs of concrete" is as silly as describing the floors as "sheets of carpeting." The floors were <u>grids of steel</u>, or a <u>mesh</u> of steel. The concrete was just a filler to provide a flat and fireproof floor. These steel beams were so thick that American steel companies supposedly could not produce them. According to FEMA and other sources, nearly all the thick steel plates were produced in Japan." (41)

Question: Was this flooring system as simplistic as the government purports?

Witness 3: Hardly. "The floor framing system for the two towers was complex and substantially more redundant than typical bar joint floor systems." (46)

Question: Did the central core of each tower depend on anything else for support?

Witness 3: No. "They were anchored directly to the bedrock, and did not depend on floor diaphragms for support." (18)

Question: Okay, now that we know each central core was a free-standing entity, let's turn our attention to the external perimeter of each building. How were these constructed?

Witness 3: "The external skeleton was a lattice work of structural steel elements." (34)

Question: And how about the outer façade that everyone saw when peering up from the street?

Witness 3: "The external façade was constructed of aluminum and glass." (34)

Question: Was this outer structure attached to the central core?

Witness 3: Yes, "the perimeter columns were connected to the core by means of steel bar-joist trusses in the concrete floors." (46)

Question: We're going to speak of these trusses later on, but before doing so, ponder this: was there a lot of material used in the construction of the towers that could easily catch fire?

Witness 3: Absolutely not. "None of the building materials provided much fuel for fire. The only readily available fuel would have been some of the decorative construction materials, such as carpet and draperies, and whatever was provided by the building's tenants, primarily office furniture and paper products." (34)

Question: We are going to cover this subject in much greater detail later, but for the time being, would these materials have been enough to create roaring fires capable of collapsing the towers?

Witness 3: "None of it would have come close to sustaining a fire of sufficient intensity to cause the collapse of the towers." (34)

Question: Were there also sprinkler systems?

Witness 3: Yes, the towers were "retrofitted with fire-sprinkler systems capable of handling routine office fires." (34)

Question: So, what we essentially have are steel and concrete towers that became at their time of construction the tallest buildings in the world – quite literally a showcase for America. How well were these buildings put together?

Witness 3: Because these buildings were, as you said, a showcase of sorts, "We can imagine that the architects, engineers, builders and inspectors would be very careful to over-build every aspect of the building. If one bolt was calculated to serve, you can bet that three or four were used." (4) Also, technically speaking, "a structural member must be physically capable of holding three times the maximum load that will ever be required of it." (4) But "the steel used in those buildings must have been able to hold five times its normal load." (46) "So, breaking strength = 5x working strength. And, given that none of the floors was holding a grand piano sale or an elephant convention that day [9-11], it is unlikely that any of them were loaded to the maximum." (4)

Question: What exactly does this mean?

Witness 3: According to Dr. Thomas Eager, a professor of materials engineering at MIT, "the steel in the towers could have collapsed only if it was heated to the point at which it lost 80% of its strength, which would be about 1300 degrees F." (46)

Question: We're going to ask each of the jurors to keep this 1300 degree figure in mind, for it will become crucial in our upcoming testimony. Now, moving along, are the statements you're giving unique only to you, or have they been confirmed by others?

Witness 3: Robert McNamara, president of the engineering firm McNamara and Salvia, said in the October 9, 2001 edition of *Scientific American*, "Nowadays, they just don't build them as tough as the World Trade Center." (46)

Question: Give us an example.

Witness 3: "The structures were so stable that the top of each tower only swayed three feet in a high wind." (4)

Question: Please elaborate.

Witness 3: "These buildings were indeed solidly constructed. Proof of this lies in the fact that they stood for thirty years in winds which sometimes reached hurricane force. Would one-quarter mile high buildings which relied solely on the integrity of weak trusses and 5/8" bolts have stood for thirty years?" (13)

Question: Have any of those involved in the construction of the towers weighed in on its design?

Witness 3: As a matter of fact, they have. Hyman Brown, the World Trade Center's construction manager and University of Colorado civil engineering professor, said of the towers: "They were over-designed to withstand almost anything, including hurricanes, high winds, bombings and an airplane hitting it." (27)

Question: Did the other designers concur?

Witness 3: Aaron Swirski, a WTC architect, told *Jerusalem Post Radio* after the attacks: "The towers were designed around the eventuality to survive this kind of attack." (27) Also, Leslie Robertson, the project's structural engineer, stated, "I designed it for a 707 to hit it. That was the largest plane at that time. I believe that the building could probably sustain multiple impacts of jet liners because this structure is like the mosquito netting on your screen door, this intense grid, and the plane is just a pencil puncturing that screen netting. It really does nothing to the screen netting." (13)

Question: Some people claim that a 767 jetliner which hit the towers is much larger, and therefore more destructive than a 707, which these structures were designed to sustain injury against. Is this sentiment accurate?

Witness 3: No it is not. *Global Research* compared these two jetliners, and here is what they discovered. (28)

- Maximum takeoff weight: Boeing 707 – 336,000 pounds
- Maximum takeoff weight: Boeing 767 – 395,000 pounds
    - a 15 % difference
- Wingspan for a Boeing 707 – 146 feet
- Wingspan for a Boeing 767 – 156 feet
    - a 7 % difference
- Length of a Boeing 707 – 153 feet
- Length of a Boeing 767 – 159 feet
    - 4 % difference

- Maximum fuel capacity: Boeing 707 – 23,000 gallons
- Maximum fuel capacity: Boeing 767 – 23,980 gallons
    - a 4 % difference

$$-14000 \text{ gals} \times 8 \text{ lb/gal} = 112000$$

$$\begin{array}{r} 395000 \\ -\ 112000 \\ \hline 283000 \text{ lbs} \end{array}$$

- Cruising speed for a Boeing 707 – 607 mph

- Cruising speed for a Boeing 767 – 530 mph

- a 13% difference

Question: What do these numbers tell us about the two jetliners?

Witness 3: "The Boeing 707 and 767 are very similar aircraft, with the main differences being that the 767 is slightly heavier and more fuel-efficient, and the 707 is faster." (28)

Question: Before we get to the final analysis of these two planes in relation to the twin towers, approximately how much fuel were the Boeing 767's carrying on the morning of September 11, 2001?

Witness 3: Since "the actual aircraft involved in the World Trade Center impacts were only flying from Boston to Los Angeles, they consequently would have been nowhere near fully fueled on takeoff. The aircraft would have carried just enough fuel for the aircraft with some safety factor." (28)

Question: And why is that?

Witness 3: "Carrying excess fuel means higher fuel bills." (28)

Question: How much fuel, then, were the planes carrying when they hit the towers?

Witness 3: "Government sources estimate that each of the Boeing 767's had approximately 10,000 gallons of unused fuel on board at the times of impact." (28)

Question: With all of this information in mind, can we determine if the damage of a 767 would be similar to that of a 707, which the towers were designed to sustain an impact from?

Witness 3: Yes, the calculation is as follows: (28)

- Thrust to weight ratio for a Boeing 707 is 4 x 18,000/336,000 = 0.214286

- Thrust to weight ratio for a Boeing 767 is 2 x 31,500/395,000 = 0.159494

"Since the Boeing 707 had a higher thrust to weight ratio, it would be traveling faster on takeoff and on landing. And, since the Boeing 707 would have started from a faster cruise speed, it would be traveling faster in a dive. So, in all the likely variations of an accidental impact with the WTC, the Boeing 707 would be traveling faster. In terms of impact damage, this higher speed would more than compensate for the slightly lower weight of the Boeing 707." (28)

Question: Is there a formula to determine the amount of energy that would be imparted to the towers?

Witness 3: Yes, it is as follows: (28)

- kinetic energy released by the impact of a Boeing 707 at cruise speed — 0.5 x 336,000 x $(890)2/32.174$ = 4.136 billion foot pounds of force

- kinetic energy released by the impact of a Boeing 767 at cruise speed — 0.5 x 395,000 x $(777)2/32.174$ = 3.706 billion foot pounds of force

Question: I realize that the previous formula is quite complex, but in simplest terms, what can be concluded from it?

Witness 3: "At cruising speed, a Boeing 707 would smash into the WTC with about 10% <u>more energy</u> than would the slightly heavier Boeing 767." (28)

Question: Which is to say?

Witness 3: "Under normal flying conditions, a Boeing 707 would do <u>more</u> damage than a Boeing 767!" (28)

Question: And once again, to reiterate, the towers were designed to withstand the impact of a 707?

Witness 3: Correct.

Question: Then they would have been able to withstand the impact of a Boeing 767, which is what struck it?

Witness 3: Correct.

Question: Before we close, how were the towers constructed in comparison to those of today?

Witness 3: Here is an exact quote from the BBC: "Newer skyscrapers are constructed using cheaper methods. But this building was magnificent, say experts." (39)

Question: Finally, what did FEMA determine about the WTC's design?

Witness 3: "Their study did not reveal any specific structural features that would be regarded as substandard, and, in fact, many structural and fire protection features of the design and construction were found to be superior to the maximum code requirements." (37)

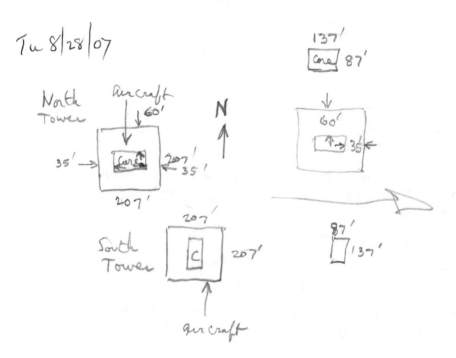

WITNESS FOUR

Impact

Now that we know the government's official version of events, as well as how the towers were constructed, the next logical step is to briefly examine what happened upon impact when each plane struck the World Trade Center towers.

Question: As we have already determined, a Boeing 767 is quite similar to a Boeing 707, from which the towers were designed to withstand impact. In terms of maximum damage infliction, was a Boeing 767 the optimal choice of aircraft?

Witness 4: No it wasn't.

Question: If the supposed hijackers had wanted to ensure the maximum amount of damage, what type of airplane would they have selected?

Witness 4: A Boeing 747.

Question: Why is that?

Witness 4: "Boeing 747's weigh more than twice as much, they can carry more than twice the fuel, and they travel faster than the Boeing 767. Consequently, Boeing 747's would have caused much more death and destruction than 767's." (28)

Question: Very well. Now, briefly describe the types of hits each tower took on the morning of 9-11.

East West Core longest dimension

Witness 4: "The North tower took a direct hit, perpendicular to the core, while the South tower took more of an angular hit, almost parallel to the core structure." (5)

North South Core longest dimension

Question: I ask the jurors to please keep this vital information in mind, for it will be crucial in our upcoming testimony. In the meantime, since the second tower – the South Tower – was hit at such an extreme angle, what happened to the fuel it was carrying?

Witness 4: "Flight 175's bad approach angle meant the jet fuel burst out of the building and exploded outside." (23)

Question: This was the huge fireball we all saw on television?

Witness 4: Yes.

Question: And since a good portion of the fuel burned outside the building, where else could it go?

Witness 4: This implies that a good deal of it didn't go inside the South Tower.

Question: Now, in regard to the steel columns and massive core which we questioned a previous witness about, what effect did the impact have on these towers?

Witness 4: Thomas Eager, who was featured in NOVA's *How the Towers Fell* documentary as a supporter of the government's claims, admitted, "The impact of the airplanes would have been insignificant because the number of columns lost on the initial impact was not large and the loads were shifted to remaining columns in this highly redundant structure." (46) Likewise, Eric Hufschmid, author of *Painful Questions*, added, "Within a few dozen seconds after the plane crash, the North Tower was quiet, stable, and motionless." (46)

Question: Would the crashing planes have had much effect on the central core?

Witness 4: "The steel beams bearing most of the load were located in the center of the tower, and thus most of the metal from the plane would not have hit the central steel beams, which would thus have remained largely undamaged by the impact." (23)

Question: A previous witness – Leslie Robertson, who was the WTC's structural engineer – compared the plane's impact to a pencil piercing a mosquito net. Is this an accurate assessment?

Witness 4: It is. "The speed of a projectile determines whether the impact damage is localized or spread across a large area. The faster the projectile, the more localized the damage." (28)

Question: Please give us an example.

Witness 4: Examples of this concept would be "the driving of a nail through a piece of wood, or firing a bullet into a fencepost. Both are done at speed and thus do only local damage." (28)

Question: So what happens to the material that is not in direct proximity to the high-speed projectile?

Witness 4: "In both of these examples, the wood just a centimeter or two from the impact point is essentially undamaged." (28)

Question: Would this notion also apply to the World Trade Center?

Witness 4: Yes, "the aircraft impacts were at great speed and the damage <u>localized</u>." (28)

Question: Could you tell us precisely how you define "localized"?

Witness 4: Localized: "confined or restricted to a particular locality ... fixed in one area or part." (Source: www.dictionary.com)

Question: To close, then, this definition would not in any way contain the word "widespread" — as in "widespread damage."

Witness 4: No, it would not.

WITNESS FIVE
Jet Fuel Fires

The government's official version of events focuses primarily on the burning jet fuel which supposedly brought down the towers.

Question: At what time did Flight 11 hit WTC 1, the North Tower?

Witness 5: "At 8:46 a.m." (41)

Question: And at what time did Flight 175 crash into WTC 2, the South Tower?

Witness 5: "At 9:03 a.m." (41)

Question: As we mentioned in earlier testimony, according to government sources, these jetliners were carrying approximately 10,000 gallons of fuel upon takeoff. What happened to this jet fuel upon impact with each of the towers?

Witness 5: "The jet fuel created spectacular fireballs when the airplanes crashed, but within a few minutes most of the flames vanished." (41)

Question: We'll cover this area in more depth a little later, but for the time being, why did the flames vanish so quickly?

Witness 5: "The lack of flames is an indication that the fires were small, and the dark smoke is an indication that the fires were suffocating." (41)

Question: And why is that?

Witness 5: "The soot and lack of flames can be used as evidence that the fires were suffocating from such a lack of oxygen that they were not capable of damaging such a massive steel structure." (41)

Question: Of course the government would like us to believe that this fire was a raging inferno. How would you describe it?

Witness 5: "The fire in the World Trade Center was an ordinary smoldering office fire." (7)

Question: Very well. In regard to the second tower that was hit – WTC 2 – we can see from the video that because Flight 175 hit very much off-center – in fact, right on the corner of the building – what happened to most of the fuel it was carrying?

Witness 5: "Most of Flight 175's fuel burned outside WTC 2." (11) "The vast majority of fuel from the second aircraft was ejected out the side of the building, where it burned up immediately in a massive fireball." (34)

Question: To be perfectly clear, why did this occur?

Witness 5: "Whoever was controlling the plane did not manage a direct hit; but rather the plane hit the tower toward a corner and at a shallow angle. Thus, comparatively little of the jet fuel entered the building." (23)

Question: And this phenomenon is directly due to the trajectory of impact with the tower?

Witness 5: "As Flight 175 disappeared inside the South Tower, it burst like a paper bag full of water. The thousands of pounds of jet fuel were liberated to follow a path dictated by the momentum of what had once been an aircraft." (25) So, "it exploded OUTSIDE in the open air over the street." (25)

Question: Once again, we'll cover this topic more fully later in our testimony, but for now, how long were flames visible from the second tower that was hit – the South Tower?

Witness 5: "Flames were visible in the South Tower for only a few minutes after the impact." (45)

Question: And did the fire spread rapidly to consume a large portion of the tower?

Witness 5: "The fire never spread beyond the impact zone, and then appeared to diminish over time." (45)

Question: Can your response be proven by photographs taken on the morning of 9-11?

Witness 5: Yes. "Photos show the spectacular flames vanished quickly, and then the fire remained restricted to one area of the tower." (41)

Question: The government wants us to believe that the fires created such a massive amount of heat that it crippled these steel buildings. But did the fires actually spread throughout the towers?

Witness 5: The fire did not "spread beyond its initial starting location. The photos show that not even one floor in the South Tower was above the ignition temperature of plastic and paper!" (41)

Question: Okay, as mentioned earlier, let's examine how quickly the fuel inside each plane burned off. To begin, please describe the qualities inherent to liquid fuel.

Witness 5: "Liquid fuel does not burn hot for long. Liquid fuel evaporates or boils as it burns, and the vapor burns as it boils off. If the ambient temperature passes the flash point of the fuel and oxygen is plentiful, the process builds to an explosion that consumes the fuel." (4)

Question: And approximately how long would it have taken for this fuel to either burn off or explode into a fireball?

Witness 5: "The jet fuel fires were brief. Most of the jet fuel would have burnt off or evaporated within thirty seconds, and all of it within 2-3 minutes." (28)

Question: And if the plane was carrying 10,000 gallons of fuel, how long would the entire burn-off process take?

Witness 5: "If all 10,000 gallons of fuel were evenly spread across a single building floor as a pool, it would be consumed by fire in less than five minutes." (28)

Question: Would anything else have occurred in relation to the fuel?

Witness 5: "The energy from the jet fuel not absorbed by the concrete and steel within this brief period would have been vented to the outside world." (28)

Question: Does the 'official' FEMA report concur with these findings?

Witness 5: Yes, in Chapter Two of the FEMA report, they write, "The large quantity of jet fuel carried by each aircraft ignited upon impact into each building. A significant portion of this fuel was consumed immediately in the ensuing fireballs. The remaining fuel is believed either to have flowed down through the buildings or to have burned off within a few minutes of the aircraft impact. The heat produced by this burning jet fuel does not by itself appear to have been sufficient to initiate the structural collapses." (37)

Question: The FEMA report does add, though, that the burning jet fuel spread across several floors of the building, ignited the building's contents, and thus caused simultaneous fires across several floors of both buildings. The first area I'd like to cover in regard to this statement is the temperature of the fires. Did it actually reach 2000 degrees Fahrenheit?

Witness 5: "This is impossible, because 1517 degrees F is the maximum temperature of hydrocarbon fires burning in the atmosphere without pressurization or pre-heating." (18)

Question: In other words, the only way it could get hotter than that temperature was if there was pre-mixed fuel and air which could produce blue flames, similar to that used by steel-cutters?

Witness 5: Correct.

Question: Let's make the physics of fire temperatures perfectly clear then.

Witness 5: "The melting point of steel is 2,795 degrees F. The highest temperature you can achieve by burning hydrocarbons in the atmosphere without pressurization or preheating of the air is 1517 degrees F, and that's when you have pre-mixed fuel and air – the kind of blue flame you get with a gas stove." (19)

Question: Would the type of flames indicative of a structural fire be hotter or cooler than what you've described?

Witness 5: "Diffuse flames of the type you have in building fires are far cooler" than those mentioned above. (19)

Question: And oxygen-starved flames?

Witness 5: "Oxygen-starved flames are far cooler still." (19)

Question: FEMA's *Building Performance Assessment* report states that temperatures at the crash site reached 1700-2000 degrees F – so intense that they could have melted the steel girders. Is this an accurate assessment?

Witness 5: Author and researcher Eric Hufschmid has stated, "If FEMA's temperature estimates are correct, the interiors of the towers were furnaces capable of casting aluminum and glazing pottery." (41)

Question: Yet if we look at photographs taken on the morning of 9-11, we see a blonde-haired woman standing inside one of the towers at the impact point.

Witness 5: Yes, "in the center of the impact hole there is a blonde standing there, leaning to the right. One must contemplate just how cool the pre-collapse temperatures were, at the impact – and presumably the hottest – point." (16)

Question: Did firemen on the scene feel that the flames were out of control?

Witness 5: "Firemen were able to work for an extended period of time in close proximity and believed the fires they encountered were manageable." (43)

Question: We'll cover the firemen in much greater depth later, but from what we've encountered thus far; this is a far stretch from what the government has described, isn't it?

Witness 5: Kevin Ryan, laboratory director for a South Bend, Indiana firm named Environmental Health Laboratories, Inc – which is, by the way, a subsidiary of Underwriters Laboratories, Inc – wrote that "the institute's preliminary reports suggest the WTC's supports were probably exposed to fires no hotter than 500 degrees – only half the 1,100-degree temperature needed to forge steel, and the 3,000 degrees needed to melt bare steel with no fire-proofing." (14)

Question: I'm glad you mentioned Mr. Ryan, for we'll examine his words more fully later in this trial. But for the time being, what else did he conclude?

Witness 5: Ryan wrote in an e-mail to Frank Gayle, deputy chief of the National Institute of Science and Technology's metallurgy division, that, "this story just does not add up." He continued, "If steel from those buildings did soften or melt, I'm sure we can all agree that this was certainly not due to jet fuel fires of any kind, let alone the briefly burning fires in those towers." (14)

Question: I would like to recall the BBC's official version of events, specifically a statement made by structural engineer Chris Wise: "There's nothing on earth that could survive those temperatures with that amount of fuel burning." Is his statement accurate?

Witness 5: No, because "we are told that the fires were unimaginably hot infernos – never mind that they were putting out black smoke and you couldn't even see flames for the most part." (19)

Question: Do you have any other areas of contention with the 'official' BBC version of events?

Witness 5: Yes, they stated that 24,000 gallons of aviation fuel melted the steel, "when we have clearly seen from government reports that each plane was carrying, at maximum, 10,000 gallons." (39)

Question: We've referred to photographic evidence in relation to the fires. What more can you tell us about the vast array of photos?

Witness 5: "The photos show the fire was not even powerful enough to crack glass! Why do photos show only sooty smoke and black holes? Why is there no evidence of an intense fire in any photograph?" (41)

Question: You mean, of course, after the intense fireball?

Witness 5: Yes.

Question: In your opinion, these photographs don't pan out with the official government story?

Witness 5: "For the official theory to be credible the fires in the towers must have been moderately hot; they must have been large fires, spreading throughout the buildings; and they must have burned for a considerable length of time. All the available evidence suggests that the opposite was the case." (46)

Question: What is the best indication that these buildings were not consumed by raging infernos?

Witness 5: When we look at the photographs, we see that "the dark smoke and lack of flames are an indication that the fires did not have enough oxygen to burn properly." (41)

Question: Which would mean?

Witness 5: "There were no intense fires for the simple reason that there was no fuel available to feed such blazes." (34)

Question: When the South Tower was hit, what was occurring in the first tower – WTC 1?

Witness 5: "In the North Tower, impacted just 16½ minutes earlier, the flames had already died down and copious amounts of thick, black smoke were pouring out of the building, indicating a smoldering, oxygen-deprived fire, not a raging inferno. The truth is; there were no concentrated, intense fires burning in either of the towers, as photographs, videotape, survivor accounts and the firefighter audiotapes all amply document." (34) "The fires had been burning for only 16 minutes, but already most of the flames had vanished." (41) "This skyscraper was not a towering inferno by the time 16 minutes had passed." (46)

Question: Why?

Witness 5: "The lack of flames is an indication that the fires were small, and the dark smoke is an indicator that the fires were suffocating." (46)

Question: When we look at photos of the North Tower a few minutes after impact, we only see black holes at the impact point. Why?

Witness 5: "There is a reason these holes are black; the reason is there is <u>no fire near the hole</u>." (41)

Question: Do we know why?

Witness 5: The North Tower fires were suffocating because "the windows were sealed shut, so the only oxygen available to the fire was whatever blew in from the few broken windows and the hole created by the airplane." (41)

Question: With the result being what?

Witness 5: "Only one floor in the North Tower appeared completely on fire. The fires on the other floors did not spread throughout the floor, nor were flames visible in many windows. Rather, the flames <u>diminished over time</u>. This implies the air temperature on all but one floor of the North Tower was <u>below the ignition temperature of plastic and</u>

paper. Therefore, only the columns in that one floor are likely to have reached high temperatures." (41)

Question: In all fairness, could there have been any other way for the fires to have reached the inferno stage, such as the core columns acting as a chimney?

Witness 5: "If one cares to argue that the core structure was acting as a chimney, it is necessary to realize that any catastrophic temperatures which 'chimneyed' would have caused the contents of the upper floors to burn violently – which is not seen in the images." (16)

Question: The smoke we see then is indicative of what?

Witness 5: Again, "relatively cool temperatures." (16)

Question: Others have claimed that jet fuel flowed down the elevator shafts, and thus spread fire throughout the towers. Is this accurate?

Witness 5: "The Naudet Brothers videotape demonstrates the lack of any lobby smoke to suggest any amount of jet fuel pouring down the single elevator shaft and burning." (16)

Question: To clarify; were the WTC elevators one long continuous shaft?

Witness 5: No. "It must be noted that the WTC towers had three independent elevator levels, with only one elevator shaft going to the top." (16)

Question: So jet fuel couldn't spill unabated from top to bottom down a single elevator shaft?

Witness 5: Absolutely not. "The only top-to-bottom avenue for central destruction was the 47 core steel columns." (16)

Question: So, if the jet fuel was no longer burning after a minute or two, what does this indicate?

Witness 5: "The towers were billowing copious amounts of thick, black smoke indicative not of raging infernos, but of low intensity, smoldering office fires." (35)   "The great explosions on impact had consumed all the jet fuel in seconds. Now it was plastic fixtures, cabling and internal partitioning that were burning; or, smoldering to be more precise." (25)

Question: Were there any other flammable materials inside the towers?

Witness 5: "Carpets, wallpaper, occasional desks – nothing else in that office would produce those temperatures." (4)

Question: Would thick, flammable walls have been a significant contributor?

Witness 5: No. "The WTC floors were open-planned – there were no solid walls." (11)

Question: Could the central core columns, constructed almost entirely of concrete and high-quality steel, create massive infernos?

Witness 5: "We know that the jet fuel fire was too brief to heat them appreciably." (28)

Question: Why is that?

Witness 5: "The central core area contained only lift shafts and stairwells. It contained very little flammable material." (28)

Question: Which means?

Witness 5: "The core columns could only have been heated by the office fire burning in the adjacent region. Consequently, the core columns would have never gotten hot enough to fall." (28)

Question: And how do we know that?

Witness 5: "We already know this because they did not fall in the 1975 WTC office fire." (28)

Question: Did FEMA's final report concur with this analysis?

Witness 5: In Chapter Two of their final report, FEMA wrote, "It is well known that the maximum temperature that can be reached by a non-stoichiometric hydrocarbon burn – that is, hydrocarbons like jet fuel burning in air – is 1520 degrees F. The WTC fires were fuel rich, as evidenced by the thick black smoke, and thus did not reach anywhere near this upper limit of 1520 degrees F. In fact, the WTC fires would have burned at, or below, temperatures typical in office fires." (37)

Question: Did they comment any further?

Witness 5: Yes. "A significant portion of the jet fuel was consumed immediately in the ensuing fireballs. The remaining fuel is believed either to have flowed down the buildings or to have burned off within a few minutes of the aircraft impact. The heat produced by this burning jet fuel does not by itself appear to have been sufficient to initiate the structural collapses." (37)

Question: And when the South Tower fell at 9:59 a.m., after burning for only 56 minutes, what did we see?

Witness 5: "All black smoke." (17)

Question: What did the few survivors who managed to escape from the upper floors say about these fires?

Witness 5: What follows is a brief synopsis:

Stanley Clark – a survivor from the 84th floor of WTC 2 – "You could see through the wall and the cracks and see flames just, just licking up. Not a roaring inferno, just quiet flames licking up and smoke sort of eking through the wall." (11) (17)

Donovan Cowan – in an open elevator on the 78th floor Sky-Lobby – "We went into the elevator. As soon as I hit the button, that's when there was a big boom. We both got knocked down. I remember feeling this intense heat. The doors were still open. The heat lasted for maybe 15 to 20 seconds I guess. Then it stopped." (28)

Ling Young – 78th floor office – "Only in my area were people alive, and the people alive were from my office. I figured that out later because I sat around in there for 10 or 15 minutes. That's how I got so burned." (28)

Question: If someone were on the 78th floor of WTC 2 in the middle of a raging inferno that structural engineer Chris Wise described as "Nothing on earth could survive those temperatures" – would somebody be able to sit around for 10-15 minutes, then ultimately escape?

Witness 5: "Thomas Eager claims temperatures were hot enough to cause the trusses of the South Tower to fall, but here we have eyewitnesses stating that temperatures were cool enough for them to walk away." (28)

Question: Yes, remember the photograph of the blonde woman standing inside the World Trade Center at its impact point. Likewise, what did firemen on the scene have to say about these fires?

Witness 5: "Cool temperatures in the collision area were also confirmed by an audiotape indicating that firefighters reached the area of the crash damage in the South Tower and reported survivable temperatures there." (6)

Question: How close to the fires did these firemen get?

Witness 5: *The New York Times* recently revealed "that at least two men had reached the 78th floor Sky Lobby of the South Tower." (40)

Question: And what did they do upon reaching this area?

Witness 5: "The firefighters reported on the fires and casualties they encountered and began evacuating the survivors." (40)

Question: Who were these firemen?

Witness 5: "Battalion Chief Orio J. Palmer, who was organizing the evacuation of injured people, and Fire Marshal Ronald P. Bucca." (40)

Question: Did these men survive?

Witness 5: "Both men died in the collapse." (40)

Question: How do we know these details?

Witness 5: "A tape of radio conversations between firefighters exists, but only relatives of the dead men have been allowed to hear it." (28)

Question: Why is that?

Witness 5: "The United States Department of Justice has ordered secrecy measures to keep the contents of a 'lost tape' of firefighter's voices at the World Trade Center from being made public." (40)

Question: Do we know why?

Witness 5: "The reason for the secrecy surrounding the 78-minute audiotape is because it evidently debunks the accepted explanation that intense jet fuel fires melted the towers' steel beams and caused the collapses." (40)

Question: Do we know exactly what is on those audiotapes?

Witness 5: Yes we do.

Question: And we will divulge their contents in a few minutes. But first, what have those people said who have listened to these tapes?

Witness 5: The widow of firefighter Orio Palmer said, "I didn't hear fear, I didn't hear panic." (40) Also, a reporter from *The New York Times* wrote, "The voices of the firefighters showed no panic, no sense that events were racing beyond their control. At that point, the building would be standing for just a few more minutes, as the fire was weakening the structure on the floors above him. Even so, Chief Palmer could only see two pockets of fire, and called for a pair of engine companies to fight them." (40)

Question: Being that these aforementioned firemen reached the crash site, how would you characterize this situation?

Witness 5: That these "veteran firefighters had a coherent plan for putting out two pockets of fire indicates they judged the blazes to be manageable." (43)

Question: Does this correspond to the government's version of events that it was a raging inferno?

Witness 5: No. "These reports from the scene of the crash provide crucial evidence debunking the government's claims that a raging steel-melting inferno led to the tower's collapse." (43)

Question: What can you tell us about the huge discrepancy between FEMA's official report and what the firemen said on this audiotape?

Witness 5: According to Eric Hufschmid, "If FEMA's estimates are correct; the interiors of the towers were furnaces capable of casting aluminum and glazing pottery. Yet the voices on the tape prove that several firefighters were able to work without fear for an extended period of time at the point of the crash, and that the fires they encountered there were neither intense nor large." (40)

Question: Before examining the content of this 78-minute audiotape, please give us a lead-in.

Witness 5: "The fire within the South Tower appeared so manageable that NYFD Battalion Chief Orio J. Palmer asked for more engines and firefighters at 9:48 am, eleven minutes before the tower began to explode. Having reached the 78th floor Sky Lobby with Fire Marshal Ronald P. Bucca, Palmer reported two pockets of fire." (45)

Question: If they felt the building was going to collapse, was it official company policy to report such an impending danger to prevent other firemen from approaching the scene?

Witness 5: "They would have been the ones reporting this information, but instead they reported on isolated fires immediately before the building's collapse." (10)

Question: Did firefighters other than Palmer and Bucca reach the 78th floor?

Witness 5: Yes. Kevin Flynn of *The New York Times* reported this conversation from the audiotape. It is Lieutenant Joseph G. Leavey of Ladder Company 15 telling Palmer: "Orio, we're on 77, but we're in the B stairway. Trapped in here. We got to put some fire out to get to you." (28)

Question: So more than one battalion reached what the government has described as a raging inferno?

Witness 5: Correct.

Question: And what time was this?

Witness 5: "9:56 a.m." (28)

Question: Three minutes before the South Tower collapsed?

Witness 5: Correct.

Question: Let's play a portion of the audiotape:

Orio Palmer: "Battalion Seven ... Ladder 15, we've got two isolated pockets of fire. We should be able to knock it down with two lines. Radio that, 78th floor numerous 10- 45 code ones."

Joseph Leavey: "Chief, what stair you in?"

Orio Palmer: "South stairway Adam, South Tower."

Joseph Leavey: "Floor 78?"

Orio Palmer: "Ten-four, numerous civilians. We're gonna need two engines up here."

Orio Palmer: "I'm going to need two of your firefighters Adam stairway to knock down two fires. We have a house line stretched. We could use some water on it, knock it down, kay."

Joseph Leavey: "Alright, ten-four. We're coming up the stairs. We're on 77 now in the B stair. I'll be right to you." (45) (10)

Question: From this audiotape, why do you feel that Lieutenant Leavey was heading directly to meet Battalion Chief Palmer?

Witness 5: "The reason that the firefighters bolted up the stairwell was that they were totally certain that there was no danger of collapse. They had no fear; and one may go to the transcripts of the radio traffic for evidence of their associated faith and courage." (16)

Question: In your opinion, why do you feel they had such confidence?

Witness 5: "Steel buildings just don't collapse from fire damage." (16)

Question: How do we know this?

Witness 5: Because "fire has <u>never</u> caused a steel building to collapse." (41)

ARTICLE ONE
Did Burning Jet Fuel
Cause the WTC Towers to Collapse?

By this point we've seen scores of evidence casting doubt on the government's official version of events that a raging inferno – which resulted from burning jet fuel – caused the World Trade Center towers to collapse. At this point we're going to cut directly to the chase and determine exactly how hot this burning jet fuel got.

THE JET FUEL: HOW HOT DID IT HEAT THE WORLD TRADE CENTER?

Vancouver Independent Media Center

February 27, 2003

Imagine that the entire quantity of jet fuel from the aircraft was injected into just one floor of the World Trade Center, that the jet fuel burnt with perfect efficiency, that no hot gases left this floor, and that no heat escaped this floor by conduction. With these ideal assumptions we calculate the maximum temperature that this one floor could have reached.

"The Boeing 767 is capable of carrying up to 23,980 gallons of fuel and it is estimated that, at the time of impact, each aircraft had approximately 10,000 gallons of unused fuel on board (compiled from Government sources)." -- Quote from the FEMA report into the collapse of WTC One and Two (Chapter Two).

Since the aircraft were only flying from Boston to Los Angeles, they would have been nowhere near fully fueled on takeoff (the aircraft have a maximum range of 7,600 miles). They would have carried just enough fuel for the trip, together with some safety factor. Remember that carrying excess fuel means higher fuel bills and less paying passengers. The aircraft would have also burnt some fuel between Boston and New York.

What we propose to do is to pretend that the entire 10,000 gallons of jet fuel was injected into just one floor of the World Trade Center, that the jet fuel burnt with the perfect quantity of oxygen, that no hot gases left this floor, and that no heat escaped this floor by conduction. With these ideal assumptions (none of which were met in reality) we will calculate the maximum temperature that this one floor could have reached. Of course, on that day, the real temperature rise of any floor due to the burning jet fuel would have been considerably lower than the rise that we calculate, but this estimate will enable us to demonstrate that the "official" explanations are lies.

Note that a gallon of jet fuel weighs about 3.1 kilograms, hence 10,000 gallons weighs 10,000 x 3.1 = 31,000 kgs.

Jet fuel is a colorless, combustible, straight run petroleum distillate liquid. Its principal uses are as an ingredient in lamp oils, charcoal starter fluids, jet engine fuels and insecticides.

It is also known as fuel oil # 1, kerosene, range oil, coal oil, and aviation fuel.

It is comprised of hydrocarbons with a carbon range of C9 – C17. The hydrocarbons are mainly alkanes C_nH_{2n+2}, with n ranging from 9 to 17.

It has a flash point within the range 42° C - 72° C (110° F – 162° F).

And an ignition temperature of 210° C (410° F).

Depending on the supply of oxygen, jet fuel burns by one of three chemical reactions:

(1) C_nH_{2n+2} + (3n+1)/2 O_2 => n CO_2 + (n + 1) H_2O

(2) C_nH_{2n+2} + (2n+1)/2 O_2 => n CO + (n + 1) H_2O

(3) C_nH_{2n+2} + (n+1)/2 O_2 => n C + (n + 1) H_2O

Reaction (1) only occurs when jet fuel is well mixed with air before being burnt, as for example, in jet engines.

Reactions (2) and (3) occur when a pool of jet fuel burns. When reaction (3) occurs the carbon formed shows up as soot in the flame. This makes the smoke very dark.

In the aircraft crashes at the World Trade Center, the collision would have mixed the fuel with the limited amount of air available within the building, but the combustion would still have been mainly a combination of reactions (2) and (3), as the quantity of oxygen was quite restricted.

Since we do not know the exact quantities of oxygen available to the fire, we will assume that the combustion was perfectly efficient, that is, the entire quantity of jet fuel burnt via reaction (1), even though we know that this was not so. This generous assumption will give a temperature that we know will be higher than the actual temperature of the fire attributable to the jet fuel.

We need to know that the (net) calorific value of jet fuel when burnt via reaction (1) is 42-44 MJ/kg. The calorific value of a fuel is the amount of energy released when the fuel is burnt. We will use the higher value of 44 MJ/kg as this will lead to a higher maximum temperature than the lower value of 42 (and we wish to continue being outrageously generous in our assumptions).

For a cleaner presentation and simpler calculations we will also assume that our hydrocarbons are of the form C_nH_{2n}. The dropping of the 2 hydrogen atoms does not make much difference to the final result and the interested reader can easily recalculate the figures for a slightly more accurate result. So we are now assuming the equation:

(4) $C_nH_{2n} + 3n/2\ O_2 \Rightarrow n\ CO_2 + n\ H_2O$

However, this model does not take into account that the reaction is proceeding in air, which is only partly oxygen.

Dry air is 79% nitrogen and 21% oxygen (by volume). Normal air has a moisture content from 0 to 4%. We will include the water vapor and other minor atmospheric gases with the nitrogen.

So the ratio of the main atmospheric gases, oxygen and nitrogen, is 1:3.76. In molar terms:

$$Air = O_2 + 3.76\ N_2$$

Because oxygen comes mixed with nitrogen, we have to include it in the equations. Even though it does not react, it is "along for the ride" and will absorb heat, affecting the overall heat balance. Thus we need to use the equation:

(5) $C_nH_{2n} + 3n/2(O_2 + 3.76\ N_2) \Rightarrow n\ CO_2 + n\ H_2O + 5.64n\ N_2$

From this equation we see that the molar ratio of C_nH_{2n} to that of the products is:

$$C_nH_{2n} : CO_2 : H_2O : N_2\ = 1 : n : n : 5.64n\ \text{moles}$$
$$= 14n : 44n : 18n : 28 \times 5.64n\ \text{kgs}$$
$$= 1 : 3.14286 : 1.28571 : 11.28\ \text{kgs}$$
$$= 31,000 : 97,429 : 39,857 : 349,680\ \text{kgs}$$

In the conversion of moles to kilograms we have assumed the atomic weights of hydrogen, carbon, nitrogen and oxygen are 1, 12, 14 and 16 respectively.

Now each of the towers contained 96,000 (short) tons of steel. That is an average of 96,000/117 = 820 tons per floor. Let's suppose that the bottom floors contained roughly twice the amount of steel of the upper floors (since the lower floors had to carry more weight). So we estimate that the lower floors contained about 1,100 tons of steel and the upper floors about 550 tons = 550 x 907.2 ≈ 500,000 kgs. We will assume that the floors hit by the aircraft contained the lower estimate of 500,000 kgs of steel. This generously underestimates the quantity of steel in these floors, and once again leads to a higher estimate of the maximum temperature.

Each story had a floor slab and a ceiling slab. These slabs were 207 feet wide, 207 feet deep and 4 (in parts 5) inches thick and were constructed from lightweight concrete. So each slab contained 207 x 207 x 1/3 = 14,283 cubic feet of concrete. Now a cubic foot of lightweight concrete weighs 50kg, hence each slab weighed 714,150 ≈ 700,000 kgs. Together, the floor and ceiling slabs weighed some 1,400,000 kgs.

So, now we take all the ingredients and estimate a maximum temperature to which they could have been heated by 10,000 gallons of jet fuel. We will call this maximum temperature T. Since the calorific value of jet fuel is 44 MJ/kg, we know that 10,000 gallons = 31,000 kgs of jet fuel will release

31,000 x 44,000,000 = 1,364,000,000,000 Joules of energy.

This is the total quantity of energy available to heat the ingredients to the temperature T. But what is the temperature T? To find out, we first have to calculate the amount of energy absorbed by each of the ingredients.

That is, we need to calculate the energy needed to raise:

39,857 kilograms of water vapor to the temperature T° C,

97,429 kilograms of carbon dioxide to the temperature T° C,

349,680 kilograms of nitrogen to the temperature T° C,

500,000 kilograms of steel to the temperature T° C,

1,400,000 kilograms of concrete to the temperature T° C.

To calculate the energy needed to heat the above quantities, we need their specific heats. The specific heat of a substance is the amount of energy needed to raise one kilogram of the substance by one degree centigrade.

Substance	Specific Heat [J/kg*C]
Concrete	3,300
Steel	450
Nitrogen	1,038
Water Vapor	1,690
Carbon Dioxide	845

Substituting these values into the above, we obtain the following numbers of joules needed to heat the substances from 25° to T° C:

39,857 x 1,690 x (T− 25) Joules are needed to heat the water vapor from 25° to T° C,

97,429 x 845 x (T − 25) Joules are needed to heat the carbon dioxide from 25° to T° C,

349,680 x 1,038 x (T − 25) Joules are needed to heat the nitrogen from 25° to T° C,

500,000 x 450 x (T – 25) Joules are needed to heat the steel from 25° to T° C,

1,400,000 x 3,300 x (T– 25) Joules are needed to heat the concrete from 25° to T° C.

The assumption that the specific heats are constant over the temperature range from 25° to T° C is a good approximation if T turns out to be relatively small (as it does). For larger values of T this assumption once again leads to a higher maximum temperature (as the specific heat for these substances increases with temperature). We have assumed the initial temperature of the surroundings to be 25° C. The quantity, (T - 25° C), is the temperature rise.

So the amount of energy needed to raise one floor to the temperature T° C is:

= (39,857 x 1,690 + 97,429 x 845 + 349,680 x 1,038 +
  500,000 x 450 + 1,400,000 x 3,300) x (T - 25)

= (67,358,300 + 82,327,500 + 362,968,000 + 225,000,000 +
  4,620,000,000) x (T - 25) Joules

= 5,357,650,000 x (T - 25) Joules.

Since the amount of energy available to heat this floor is 1,364,000,000,000 Joules, we have:

5,357,650,000 x (T - 25) = 1,364,000,000,000
5,357,650,000 x T - 133,941,000,000 = 1,364,000,000,000

Therefore T = (1,364,000,000,000 +
133,941,000,000)/5,357,650,000 = 280° C (536° F).

So, if we assume a typical office fire at the WTC, then the jet fuel could have only added 280 - 25 = 255° C (at the very most) to the temperature of the fire.

Summarizing:

We have assumed that the entire quantity of jet fuel from the aircraft was injected into just one floor of the World Trade Center; that the jet fuel burnt with perfect efficiency, that no hot gases left this floor, and that no heat escaped this floor by conduction.

We have found that it is impossible that the jet fuel, by itself, raised the temperature of this floor beyond 280° C (536° F).

Now this temperature is nowhere near high enough to even begin explaining the World Trade Center Tower collapse.

ARTICLE TWO
The Kevin Ryan Letter

The collapse of the WTC

by Kevin Ryan
Underwriters Laboratories
Thursday, Nov 11, 2004

Dr. Gayle,

Having recently reviewed your team's report of 10/19/04, I felt the need to contact you directly.

As I'm sure you know, the company I work for certified the steel components used in the construction of the WTC buildings. In requesting information from both our CEO and Fire Protection business manager last year, I learned that they did not agree on the essential aspects of the story, except for one thing – that the samples we certified met all requirements. They suggested we all be patient and understand that UL was working with your team, and that tests would continue through this year. I'm aware of UL's attempts to help, including performing tests on models of the floor assemblies. But the results of these tests appear to indicate that the buildings should have easily withstood the thermal stress caused by pools of burning jet fuel.

There continues to be a number of "experts" making public claims about how the WTC buildings fell. One such person, Dr. Hyman Brown from the WTC construction crew, claims that the buildings collapsed due to fires at 2,000 F melting the steel. He states, "What caused the building to collapse is the airplane fuel...burning at 2,000 degrees Fahrenheit. The steel in that five-floor area melts." Additionally, the newspaper that quotes him says, "Just-released preliminary findings from a National Institute of Standards and

Technology study of the World Trade Center collapse support Brown's theory."

We know that the steel components were certified to ASTM E119. The time temperature curves for this standard require the samples to be exposed to temperatures around 2000 F for several hours. And as we all agree, the steel applied met those specifications. Additionally, I think we can all agree that even un-fireproofed steel will not melt until reaching red-hot temperatures of nearly 3000 F. Why Dr. Brown would imply that 2000 F would melt the high-grade steel used in those buildings makes no sense at all.

The results of your recently published metallurgical tests seem to clear things up, and support your team's August 2003 update as detailed by the Associated Press in which you were ready to "rule out weak steel as a contributing factor in the collapse." The evaluation of paint deformation and spheroidization seem very straightforward, and you noted that the samples available were adequate for the investigation. Your comments suggest that the steel was probably exposed to temperatures of only about 500 F (250 C), which is what one might expect from a thermodynamic analysis of the situation.

However the summary of the new NIST report seems to ignore your findings, as it suggests that these low temperatures caused exposed bits of the building's steel core to "soften and buckle." Additionally this summary states that the perimeter columns softened, yet your findings make clear that "most perimeter panels (157 of 160) saw no temperature above 250 C." To soften steel for the purposes of forging, normally temperatures need to be above1100 C. However, this new summary report suggests that much lower temperatures were able to not only soften the steel in a matter of minutes, but lead to rapid structural collapse.

This story just does not add up. If steel from those buildings did soften or melt, I'm sure we can all agree that this was certainly not due to jet fuel fires of any kind, let alone the briefly burning fires in those towers. That fact should be of great concern to all Americans.

Alternatively, the contention that this steel did fail at temperatures around 250 C suggests that the majority of deaths on 9/11 were due to a safety-related failure. That suggestion should be of great concern to my company.

There is no question that the events of 9/11 are the emotional driving force behind the War on Terror. And the issue of the WTC collapse is at the crux of the story of 9/11. My feeling is that your metallurgical tests are at the crux of the crux of the crux. Either you can make sense of what really happened to those buildings, and communicate this quickly, or we all face the same destruction and despair that come from global decisions based on disinformation and "chatter."

Thanks for your efforts to determine what happened on that day. You may know that there are a number of other current and former government employees that have risked a great deal to help us know the truth. I've copied one of these people on this message as a sign of respect and support. I believe your work could also be a nucleus of fact around which the truth, and thereby global peace and justice, can grow again. Please do what you can to quickly eliminate the confusion regarding the ability of jet fuel fires to soften or melt structural steel.

Kevin Ryan

Site Manager, Environmental Health Laboratories – A Division of Underwriters Laboratories

WITNESS SIX
The Towers' Collapse

As we have already proven, temperatures from burning jet fuel did not even remotely burn as intensely as the government said they did. We also seem to have another glaring discrepancy on our hands. Even though the North Tower was hit 16½ minutes before the South Tower, the South Tower, WTC 2, fell 30 minutes before WTC 1. How can that be?

Question: What time was WTC 1 – the North Tower – struck by a jetliner?

Witness 6: "8:46 a.m." (37)

Question: And at what time was WTC 2 – the South Tower – struck by a jetliner?

Witness 6: "16 ½ minutes later, at 9:03 a.m." (37)

Question: And at what time did WTC 2 collapse?

Witness 6: "9:59 a.m. – 56 minutes after impact." (37)

Question: And at what time did WTC 1 collapse?

Witness 6: "10:28 a.m. – one hour and 42 minutes after impact." (37)

Question: With this foundation in mind, let's examine some of the peculiarities found in the above scenario. First, which of the towers took a more direct hit?

Witness 6: The North Tower took "a direct impact from Flight 11." (45)

Question: And how would you describe the South Tower's impact?

Witness 6: The South Tower was struck by an "oblique impact from Flight 175." (45)

Question: Yet the South Tower stood for only 56 minutes, while the North Tower, which took a more direct hit, stood for 102 minutes. To which building was more damage done?

Witness 6: "The structural damage to the South Tower was far less severe. Fewer of its perimeter columns were damaged and very few of its core columns were compromised." (45)

Question: How about the fires? In which building were they more severe?

Witness 6: "The fires in the South Tower were far less severe, as much of United Airlines Flight 175's fuel exited the building." (45)

Question: And if smoke is any indicator of a fire's intensity, which building produced more smoke?

Witness 6: "While the North Tower continued to emit prodigious smoke, the South Tower was producing only a thin veil of black smoke by the time of its collapse." (45)

Question: And once again, what does this type of smoke indicate?

Witness 6: "Black smoke indicates a cooling, oxygen-starved fire." (45)

Question: Continuing on, how much jet fuel did the South Tower absorb in comparison to the North Tower?

Witness 6: "The South Tower took less than half the fuel load of its North Tower twin." (25)

Question: Where was the South Tower struck in comparison to the North Tower?

Witness 6: "The airplane hit about 15 floors lower in the South Tower." (41)

Question: Were the structural columns thicker or thinner the lower one went in the towers?

Witness 6: Since the South Tower was struck at a lower point, "the structural columns were <u>thicker</u> at this location." (41)

Question: And since the columns were thicker in the South Tower at the point of impact, would more or less heat have to be produced to make equally weak as in the North Tower?

Witness 6: "The South Tower would have had to produce <u>more</u> heat than the fire in the North Tower in order to raise the columns to the same temperature as in the North Tower." (41)

Question: With all this information in mind – that the South Tower experienced a less forceful hit, the structural damage was less severe, the fires were smaller, and the columns where it was hit were thicker and stronger – how long did the South Tower stand?

Witness 6: "56 minutes." (48)

Question: And how long did the North Tower stand?

Witness 6: "102 minutes." (48)

Question: Nearly twice as long. Do we have any explanation for this seeming improbability?

Witness 6: David Ray Griffin, author of *The New Pearl Harbor*, quotes Peter Meyer's article, *The World Trade Center Demolition and the So-called War on Terrorism*, specifically a section entitled, *Did the Towers Collapse on Demand*: "In both cases the fires within the buildings died down after awhile, giving off only black, sooty smoke. If the Twin Towers were deliberately demolished, and the intention was to blame the collapse on the fires ... then the latest time at which the towers could be collapsed would be just as the fires were dying down. Since the fire in the South Tower resulted from the combustion of less fuel than the fire in the North Tower, the fire in the South Tower began to go out earlier than the fire in the North Tower. Those controlling the demolition thus had to collapse the South Tower before they collapsed the North Tower." (46)

Question: Plus, what are the odds that the North Tower, the South Tower, and WTC 7 – all with different circumstances surrounding them, all collapsed to the ground in the exact same manner?

Witness 6: "A reasonable mindset finds it simply impossible for three buildings to have done an identical collapse on the same site, within hours of each other, with two different architectural styles, two distinct fire sources, with all three structures being controlled by the same individual/group." (16)

Question: And, we must remember, that never before in the history of the world had a steel building collapsed due to fire prior to 9-11. Then, on that day, how many of them collapsed?

Witness 6: Three, all within seven hours of each other, and the last one – WTC 7 – wasn't even struck by an airliner!

WITNESS SEVEN
Melting Steel

Question: In earlier testimony it was revealed that never before in the history of the world had a steel building collapsed due to fire. Is this true?

Witness 7: "The fall of the South Tower, just 56 minutes after it had been hit, marked the first time in history that a steel-framed high-rise structure had suffered a total collapse due to fire." (35)

Question: Had other steel buildings partially collapsed due to fire?

Witness 7: "Never before had such a building suffered even a partial collapse due to fire." (35)

Question: And what happened 29 minutes later after the South Tower fell?

Witness 7: "At 10:28 a.m., the North Tower became the second steel-framed high-rise structure to suffer a total collapse due to fire." (35)

Question: Also, as we'll see, WTC 7 brought the total to three steel building collapses within the span of eight hours. Anyway, moving on, since we've seen that, until 9-11, steel buildings didn't collapse due to fire, we should look at the physics of this phenomenon. My first question is: at what temperature does steel begin to melt?

Witness 7: "2,795 degrees Fahrenheit." (18)

Question: And at what temperature does steel become a molten liquid?

Witness 7: "5,182 degrees Fahrenheit." (31)

Question: Lastly, what is the melting point of aluminum?

Witness 7: "1,148 degrees Fahrenheit." (32)

Question: And the absolute highest temperature that burning jet fuel can attain is what?

Witness 7: "Jet fuel produces a maximum temperature of approximately 1800 degrees F when mixed with air in <u>perfect</u> proportions." (41)

Question: And were the conditions perfect on the morning of 9-11 to reach this maximum temperature?

Witness 7: No. "It is virtually impossible for an airplane crash to coincidentally mix the fuel and air in perfect proportions. Therefore, the temperature of the steel was <u>significantly less</u> than the maximum 1800 degrees F." (41)

Question: In fact, using a very detailed, complex scientific formula in Article 1, we calculated that the maximum floor temperature in the World Trade Center towers as a result of burning jet fuel was less than 536 degrees F. With this figure in mind, what is the variance between the melting point of steel and the actual temperatures created by this burning jet fuel?

Witness 7: 2,795 degrees minus 536 degrees equals a variance of 2,259 degrees!

Question: In other words, the actual floor temperature inside the towers created by burning jet fuel was only about 19% of that needed to melt construction grade steel?

Witness 7: Correct.

Question: Could other factors, such as burning materials inside the towers, raise the temperature to 2,795 degrees?

Witness 7: "Kerosene-based jet fuel, paper, or other combustibles normally found in towers cannot generate this much heat, especially in an oxygen-poor environment." (5)

Question: It seems we have some major discrepancies between the "official" version of events and the laws of science. First, we were told by "official sources" that molten steel – with a requisite temperature of 5,182 degrees F – actually poured out over the sides of the WTC towers. Is this possible?

Witness 7: "All the pooled jet fuel in the world won't burn hot enough to produce molten steel – under any conditions." (16)

Question: In fact, is there any evidence that the aluminum, which comprised the decorative external façade – with a melting point of only 1,148 degrees – melted?

Witness 7: "The imagery of the WTC does NOT reveal the aluminum siding of the WTC towers deforming." (16)

Question: So, if the fires did not even melt the external aluminum casing, which had much less strength, is it possible that it could have melted the much stronger construction-grade steel at the WTC core?

Witness 7: "Given both time and temperature, the outer columns should have been the structural weak link." (16)

Question: Thus, they would have been the most susceptible to fire?

Witness 7: "Given the mechanics of the heat escape, the outer columns were the most vulnerable to heat damage." (16)

Question: But since we didn't see any melting of the external aluminum casing, do you feel that the much stronger steel cores could have melted?

Witness 7: "It is difficult to imagine the fires being so hot as to cause either catastrophic or abrupt damage to the WTC vertical support structure." (16)

Question: And why is that?

Witness 7: "None of the images of the outer steel structure show the otherwise expected red-hot glow." (16)

Question: So if the steel didn't melt, and they weren't turned to a liquid molten substance, how were the steel columns weakened?

Witness 7: "All images show the outer shell mechanically destroyed, versus collapsing from a thermal cause." (16)

Question: Would a mechanical collapse include controlled demolition?

Witness 7: Yes it would.

Question: Another discrepancy involves the previously mentioned BBC report, which stated, "The fires reached 1500 degrees F – hot enough to melt steel floor supports." Was this claim accurate?

Witness 7: No. As we've already mentioned, steel melts at 2,795 degrees F.

Question: Lastly, the official version of events purports that burning fuel from the aircraft caused the WTC to collapse. Is this statement true in your opinion?

Witness 7: "No kerosene fire can burn hot enough to melt steel." (7)

Question: Let's try to put this matter into perspective. How long did it take the South Tower to collapse, with a very minor office fire burning inside of it?

Witness 7: "56 minutes." (41)

Question: And how long does it take to cook a turkey?

Witness 7: "It takes more than 56 minutes to cook a turkey." (41)

Question: And since these fires weren't spreading, how much damage could they do in 56 minutes in the South Tower?

Witness 7: "The fires were not producing much heat. Even if every column had been stripped of its fireproofing, massive steel columns will not reach high temperatures in only 56 minutes from fires that are incapable of spreading to other flammable office furnishings." (41)

Question: So, to melt steel, what type of device does one need?

Witness 7: "To melt steel you need the high temperature produced by an oxy-acetylene torch. Jet fuel burning in air – especially in an enclosed space within a building where there is much smoke and little oxygen – just won't do it." (23)

Question: What methods or devices, then, are used to melt steel?

Witness 7: Acetylene torches, bottled oxygen, electric arcs, blast furnaces, to name a few.

Question: To close, if a steelworker poured jet fuel into the tank of his acetylene torch, how effective would this be?

Witness 7: He'd be there until the end of time and wouldn't end up cutting a single piece of steel.

WITNESS EIGHT
Symmetric vs. Asymmetric Collapses

Question: What differences were there between the North Tower's collapse and that of the South Tower?

Witness 8: "The North Tower's destruction was symmetrical from its onset. But the South Tower's destruction began with its top tipping to the southeast." (45)

Question: Did the South Tower's tipping-top fall over like a tree?

Witness 8: No. "Instead of toppling, the top suddenly disintegrated and fell into the exploding tower." (45)

Question: And how far did this top-section of the South Tower actually tip over?

Witness 8: "The 35 stories of the top section continued to tip to 23 degrees past vertical." (42)

Question: How far did this tilting section extend past the remaining part of the tower which was still standing?

Witness 8: "At one point the upper segment was hanging over the edge by approximately 65 feet." (42)

Question: Would you categorize this type of collapse symmetric or asymmetric?

Witness 8: Obviously asymmetric.

Question: Which means?

Witness 8: One side of the tower collapsed and began to fall before the other side did. It wasn't a clean, even break.

Question: What would we expect of an asymmetrical collapse?

Witness 8: "Any asymmetry would allow the force of gravity to work uninhibited on the tip of the skyscraper. Thus, the top section of the skyscraper would tip and fall sideways." (7)

Question: And why is that?

Witness 8: "This follows the laws of physics. As Isaac Newton explained, once an 87 million kg object starts to tip, only an equally incredible force in the opposite direction will stop the tipping." (41)

Question: This may be a silly question, but once the top of the South Tower started tipping – all the way to 23 degrees past vertical – were there any forces at work that morning to push it back to center, say like a giant hand which came out of the clouds?

Witness 8: "There was no force up there except gravity, so there was nothing to stop the tipping." (41)

Question: Yet the top section of the tower didn't topple, did it?

Witness 8: "In theory, the 'cap' should have torn loose and independently fallen." (16)

Question: What prevented it from doing so; from falling over onto the streets of Manhattan?

Witness 8: The only thing which prevented it from tipping over was "an independent – and nearly simultaneous – collapse of the core." (16)

Question: So, when the top cap began to topple, if the core columns were suddenly destroyed, what would happen to this top section?

Witness 8: "The collapse would continue vertically – 'in formation' – with the rest of the structure." (16)

Question: Let me get this straight. At point A we have the entire structure standing still. Then at point B we have the upper section tilting to a point of 23 degrees past center. The laws of physics state – specifically Newton's First Law of

Motion – that every object in a state of uniform motion tends to remain in that state of motion unless an external force is applied to it. This means that the top should have kept following its same path and fallen over onto the street. But then, at point C – just moments later – the entire lower portion of the South Tower simultaneously collapsed – which allowed the top portion to drop <u>VERTICALLY</u> into its own footprint. Is this correct?

Witness 8: Yes. "The simultaneous 'fall' of the two sections tells a story. The 'center of gravity' of the 'cap' <u>abruptly</u> found a vertical path to the ground!" (16)

Question: So the cap started falling sideways; then suddenly fell straight down?

Witness 8: Yes.

Question: The South Tower, then, in the blink of an eye, went from an asymmetrical collapse to a symmetrical collapse. How could this be?

Witness 8: "With no other forces acting upon it, gravity and momentum should have sent the enormous block of concrete and steel crashing down <u>alongside</u> the topless tower." (34)

Question: But that's not what happened, is it?

Witness 8: "Instead of continuing to topple over, the massive block seems to have mysteriously <u>self-destructed</u>." (34)

Question: Are the laws of gravity and moving bodies being violated by this phenomenon?

Witness 8: "The law of the preservation of angular momentum says that if you have a solid object and it has an angular momentum, it will preserve that angular momentum unless acted upon by a torque." (19)

Question: Is that what happened?

Witness 8: No. "We see that it <u>doesn't</u> preserve that angular momentum. Instead, it stops rotating and starts rotating the <u>other way</u>!" (19)

Question: If we adhere to the laws of physics, would another force have to act upon this falling upper section to serve as a torque – to reverse the direction of its fall?

Witness 8: Yes.

Question: What happened as the South Tower's cap changed direction?

Witness 8: "Virtually the entire top of the South Tower had been <u>shattered</u> before it even began to fall." (19)

Question: How does this phenomenon coincide with the government's official story?

Witness 8: "It's clearly impossible according to the official theory." (19)

Question: Why?

Witness 8: Because "the top is the piston that is supposedly hammering down and crushing the rest of the building." (19)

Question: Can gravity alter a building's direction in mid-flight; then cause it to explode without an external impetus?

Witness 8: No, "not if it's already disintegrating before it's even started to fall. Gravity couldn't do that – some other form of energy had to break up the tower before it started to fall." (19)

Question: As this top section began to fall vertically, what also happened to it?

Witness 8: "Large chunks of the steel-framed building were suddenly blown-apart." (34)

Question: Tell us what happened after the top section began to tip.

Witness 8: "First we see the top of the building start to tip to one side as a monolithic block, which we would expect to continue to rotate and topple to the side. Instead, almost as soon as it starts to tip, the building below it starts to collapse, allowing it to drop straight down. There are very visible rings of explosions that start at the level where the building has begun to tip and travel rapidly down the building." (22)

Question: What ultimately happened to this top section?

Witness 8: "Instead of continuing to topple to the side, the top portion actually telescopes into itself at the same time that it sinks effortlessly into the building beneath it." (22)

Question: Did this top section remain intact as it fell vertically into the building below?

Witness 8: Remarkably, no it did not.

Question: What happened to it?

Witness 8: "Before it disappears into an immense dust cloud, we see the distance between the roof and the bottom of the upper section actually collapse to less than half its original height." (22)

Question: So it's shrinking in size while also simultaneously falling? Is this possible under the law of physics?

Witness 8: "This is especially remarkable because it is essentially in free-fall at this point." (22)

Question: Which means?

Witness 8: "There should be NO internal forces causing it to collapse upon itself." (22)

Question: What we have, then, is the top section toppling over in one direction, then dropping straight down in a free-fall, all the while exploding outward, and collapsing upon itself – all with supposedly no external force acting upon it. Could all of this have been caused by smoke and fire?

Witness 8: "Smoke and fire don't normally cause large chunks of steel-framed buildings to suddenly blow apart.

That usually only happens when explosives of some kind are involved." (34)

Question: And how would all of these bizarre circumstances have been accomplished?

Witness 8: "The only way to get the World Trade Center towers to drop straight down was to eliminate the central support structure. The best way to do that would have been to blast away a portion of each of those 47 core columns, down near where they were anchored to the bedrock, causing the entire central core of the tower to abruptly drop a given distance." (34)

Question: If we discount the possibility of a controlled demolition, what other explanations are there?

Witness 8: Well, let's look at the North Tower.

Question: The one whose top did not tip over?

Witness 8: Correct. "Since there was no tilting of the North Tower, every column in the crash zone broke in a perfectly balanced manner." (41)

Question: How is this possible considering the WTC's very strong design?

Witness 8: "There were 47 columns in the interior and 236 columns along the outside. Since the crash zone of the North Tower was near the 96th floor, the columns in this area were thinner than the columns near the ground level. However, they were still so thick that it would require a significant amount of energy to break them. How did the fire break so many columns? Did one column break, which then caused another column to break, and so on? If so, it is an amazing coincidence that the columns separated and/or snapped in such a perfectly balanced manner that the top never tilted." (41)

Question: Plus, as we have already proven, the fires never reached anywhere near a high enough temperature to melt steel. Also, in later testimony, we'll show how the government's "bolt theory" is incredible at best; and a downright lie at worst. But first, let's examine some more scientific laws. Is it reasonable to say that the towers – without any outside force except fire – would have collapsed in their own footprint?

Witness 8: No. "The collapses remained centered around their towers' vertical axes as they raced to the ground." (45)

Question: Which means what?

Witness 8: "The collapses followed what would have been the path of <u>maximal resistance</u>, unless the structure was being demolished ahead of the falling mass." (45)

Question: And why is this concept important?

Witness 8: Because "physical processes follow the path of <u>least resistance</u>." (45)

Question: Which means?

Witness 8: "Tall structures <u>topple</u> instead of crushing themselves. Without a controlled demolition, the towers' tops would have toppled, leaving standing their portions below the impact zones." (45)

Question: Please elaborate.

Witness 8: Discounting <u>demolition</u>, the telescoping collapses mean that the towers would be collapsing through <u>themselves</u> following the path of <u>most resistance</u>. That's not the way matter behaves. Even if the towers were made of toothpicks or butter, anything, they wouldn't collapse through themselves; they would topple one way or the other. And yet you see this perfect dead-centered symmetry in both collapses, even in the South Tower which started to tip, but then became symmetric. That's exactly what controlled demolition seeks to achieve in order to minimize damage to adjacent structures." (19)

Question: But the South Tower was obviously asymmetric in its initial collapse. Can an asymmetric collapse suddenly become symmetrical?

<u>**Witness 8**</u>: "Asymmetric damage cannot produce a symmetric result." (36)

Question: If the top sections of each tower would have fallen straight down without any type of controlled demolition beneath it, what would have happened?

<u>**Witness 8**</u>: "If it did not tip, it would have ground straight down through the building below. The gravitational potential energy of the upper stories would be coupled into the frame below, beginning to destroy it." (7)

Question: And what would the building below do?

<u>**Witness 8**</u>: "The frame below would deflect elastically, absorbing energy in the process of deflecting. At weak points, the metal structure would break, but the elastic energy absorbed into the entire floor would not be available to do more destruction.   Instead, it would be dissipated in vibration, acoustic noise and heat." (7)

Question: Which ultimately means?

<u>**Witness 8**</u>: "Eventually this process would grind to a halt because the gravitational potential energy of a skyscraper is nowhere near sufficient to destroy its own frame." (7)

Question: And what would we have?

<u>**Witness 8**</u>: "The lower, ground level segments of the heavy steel inner columns should have been left standing, somewhat vertically, like stray swizzle-sticks." (16)

Question: So, instead of a total demolition collapse, some of the WTC towers should have remained standing?

<u>**Witness 8**</u>: "Given that the lower columns were radically thicker steel, and obviously stronger, some of the columns should have still been standing – <u>in some significant number</u>." (16)

Question: But that's not what happened?

Witness 8: "For the WTC buildings to react the way they did, literally thousands of super heavy-duty joints and welds would have had to 'snap' at precisely the same instant." (42)

Question: Which means?

Witness 8: "All 287 columns would have to have weakened to the point of collapse at the <u>same instant</u> to cause the telescoping seen in the North Tower." (36)

Question: But as you've said, much of the inner core should have remained standing, yet both towers, plus WTC 7, were completely destroyed. Is there any explanation other than a controlled demolition?

Witness 8: "Of collapse causes other than controlled demolition, only earthquakes can cause the simultaneous damage needed to cause total collapse." (36)

Question: Were there any reported earthquakes in Manhattan that you know of on the morning of 9-11?

Witness 8: Not that I'm aware of.

WITNESS NINE
The Pancake Theory

Question: Once again, let's return to the point when each plane impacted the WTC towers. What effect did they have on these buildings, specifically the inner core?

Witness 9: "The central core was still mostly intact, especially in the South Tower, where any significant heating would have been near the corner the plane struck, and the core could not have been hit by any major parts of the plane." (22)

Question: Except for the exact moment and point of impact, how did the outer frame hold up?

Witness 9: "The outer frame is still intact at this point." (22)

Question: Our previous witnesses showed how the fires did not burn hot enough to melt the steel in these buildings. What would have happened to this steel?

Witness 9: "Before it breaks, hot steel begins to bend." (7)

Question: What happens then?

Witness 9: "This redistributes the forces in the structure and puts elastic stress on those parts that are still cool." (7)

Question: Is this a symmetric or asymmetric process?

Witness 9: "This process is asymmetric, so the structure should visibly bend before breaking." (7)

Question: Did the World Trade Center towers bend over after they caught on fire?

Witness 9: "No steel skyscraper has ever bent over in a fire." (7)

Question: Okay, since the damage to each tower was asymmetric – or uneven in that it didn't hit every section of the building with the same amount of force – what problem does this pose to the government's 'pancake' theory, where one floor fell upon another below it, and subsequently pancaked to the ground?

Witness 9: "One problem with the 'pancake' theory is that it is wholly dependent on a perfectly symmetrical failure of the floor slabs, even though the damage to the buildings was clearly asymmetrical." (35)

Question: Did the fires burn symmetrically – that is, in perfect uniformity through each building?

Witness 9: "The fires certainly did not burn uniformly throughout the damaged floors." (35)

Question: Does this scenario lend itself, then, to a perfectly symmetrical collapse?

Witness 9: "For the destruction to be complete, the collapse of the initial floor slabs would have had to be perfectly uniform; every point of connection around the perimeter of the core, and every point of connection around the exterior shell, would have had to fail at precisely the same moment in time." (35)

Question: And does this same scenario pertain to each successive floor?

Witness 9: Yes. "Each successive floor would have had to fail in exactly the same perfectly uniform manner, unerringly all the way down the line." (35)

Question: Can there be a margin of error?

Witness 9: "When the 'pancake' effect has to course through 110 floors, there isn't really any margin for error. And yet both towers, as we all know, 'pancaked' into oblivion in matching, perfectly choreographed collapses." (35)

Question: But as we've shown, the impact and damage to each tower was markedly different. How can they collapse in the exact same fashion?

Witness 9: "Remarkably enough, the two towers somehow collapsed in exactly the same manner even though the initial damage to each tower was quite different." (35)

Question: Especially the South Tower.

Witness 9: "The South Tower was hit with a more glancing blow, through the southeast corner of the building, in such a way that the plane likely did minimal damage to the tower's core." (35)

Question: Okay, hypothetically, if each floor did pancake to the ground, what would we expect to find?

Witness 9: "We are still left with no explanation of what happened to those massive concrete and steel cores." (35)

Question: Please explain.

Witness 9: "Clearly, the floor slabs were hardly the wide-open 'pancakes' depicted in deceptive media graphics. In truth, the 'pancake' theory, at best, offers only an explanation of how the floor and exterior wall sections may have collapsed. Even if such an extremely unlikely event had occurred, the end result would not have been a 60-foot-high mound of rubble." (35)

Question: What would we have seen?

Witness 9: "When the platters fell, those quarter-mile high central steel columns – at least from the ground to the fire – should have been left standing naked and unsupported in the air." (4)

Question: We should note, too, from earlier testimony that there were no flammable materials contained within these cores – only steel and concrete – so they couldn't burn. Plus, temperatures did not get high enough for them to melt. Also, what would have been the effect on the core had the floors let loose?

Witness 9: "As the floor panels let go from their mountings, the load would be relieved from the core columns – leaving them to stand/balance momentarily." (16)

Question: Did these inner columns remain standing on the morning of 9-11 after all the floors pancaked to the ground?

Witness 9: No. "In the case of both buildings, everything let go at once." (16)

Question: So, did the floors and the perimeter columns fall at the same time as these massive central cores made of enormously strong steel and concrete which had no flammable materials?

Witness 9: No. "Given the undeniable sequence, the floors fell as a CONSEQUENCE of the core column collapse, not the reverse!" (16)

Question: Why is the pancake theory a complete fallacy then?

Witness 9: "With the core columns obviously collapsing first, there had to have been something to breach the vertical integrity of the 47 steel columns – early in the collapse, not later." (16)

Question: Did this same exact process apply to WTC 1, WTC 2, and WTC 7?

Witness 9: Yes, "three buildings collapsed in this fashion." (16)

Question: And how could these steel columns have collapsed in such a total, complete, symmetrical fashion?

Witness 9: According to Peter Meyer, who is quoted in David Ray Griffin's *The New Pearl Harbor*: "This is understandable if the base of the steel columns were destroyed by explosives at the level of the bedrock. With those bases obliterated and the supporting steel columns shattered by explosions at various levels in the towers, the upper floors lost all support and collapsed to ground level in about ten seconds." (46)

Question: And how would you classify such a process?

Witness 9: "The collapse was an example of a controlled demolition, based on explosives that had been placed throughout the building." (46)

WITNESS TEN
Trusses and Bolts

Question: What is the biggest misrepresentation in FEMA's official report?

Witness 10: "FEMA's report pretends the towers would instantly self-destruct if the floors fell away." (18)

Question: And how did FEMA go about doing this?

Witness 10: "The key to this deception is hiding the strength of the core structures." (18)

Question: Okay, before we look at the Twin Towers' design, what is the government's official position on how the towers collapsed in regard to their flooring?

Witness 10: "They say the perimeter and core columns would self-destruct if the floor diaphragms collapsed. As the floors collapsed, this left tall freestanding portions of the exterior wall, and possibly central core columns. As the unsupported height of these freestanding exterior walls increased, they buckled at the bolted column splice connections, and also collapsed." (36)

Question: Were there any other theories promoted by the government?

Witness 10: Yes, materials science professor Thomas Eager advanced what is called "the zipper theory."

Question: Which is?

Witness 10: "Once you started to get angle clips – his misnomer for the steel shelves that supported the ends of the trusses – to fail, it put an extra load on other angle clips and then it unzipped around the building on that floor in a matter of seconds." (19)

Question: Where can we find this theory?

Witness 10: In NOVA's documentary, *Why the Towers Fell.*

Question: You mentioned the word 'deception' earlier in reference to the FEMA report. What are some examples of these deceptions?

Witness 10: First, in their representative floor plan, "the core column cross-sections are shown about 1/3rd their actual dimensions, and the cross-bracing core beams are not shown at all." (18)

Question: So the primary strength of these towers – their massive steel and concrete cores – has been dramatically reduced in size in their reports?

Witness 10: Yes.

Question: I realize that I'm simplifying matters, but in the NOVA special, *How the Towers Fell*, their graphics seem to imply that each floor truss was attached to the outer columns by a single bolt, and when these bolts 'popped,' the trusses fell and the outer columns began to buckle, leading to the towers' collapse. Is this actually how the towers were designed?

Witness 10: No. "It's interesting to note the deceptive techniques used by NOVA and [Thomas] Eager on its website. Their animation shows the chain reaction of collapsing trusses. It doesn't show you several other things." (19)

Question: Such as?

Witness 10: "One, there were perpendicular trusses interwoven with the trusses they show. That would have unified the entire structure and you couldn't have had this chain reaction unzipping around the building. Two, they imply that the floors merely rested on the trusses, when in fact these trusses were bolted into the pans underlying the floor slabs every few inches. Also, you'll see that the core is depicted as a series of horizontal slabs, not as vertical columns. The spandrel plates that linked the perimeter columns are also omitted." (19)

Question: Continue.

Witness 10: "A number of sub-plaza stories have solid steel beams, rather than trusses, supporting the floor slabs between the core and perimeter walls." (28)

Question: How about the WTC's flooring?

Witness 10: "The 'secret' of the World Trade Center's ability to handle wind-loading is composite flooring." (28)

Question: Please describe the difference between what the government and media told us about this flooring, and its actual design.

Witness 10: "The media coverage of the WTC collapse portrayed the concrete slabs as just sitting on the bar joists (trusses), and implied that these bar joists could just fall away from the slabs if weakened by fire." (28)

Question: And that's not the case?

Witness 10: No. "The floors were supported by an 'x-y' grid of vertical supports, not a single row of trusses, as otherwise suggested." (16) Also, "the perimeter structures (outside walls) and core structures were not free-standing." (19)

Question: Were they connected to each other?

Witness 10: "The perimeter columns were linked by horizontal spandrel plates, and the core structure was a highly cross-linked structure that was easily capable of supporting itself and several times the weight of the entire building." (19)

Question: Yet FEMA tells us the towers would immediately fall if the floors fell away. Is that a true assessment?

Witness 10: No. "The key deception is to represent the core as flimsy." And, as I said earlier, they do this by "showing the columns at about a third of their dimensions. They don't show the cross-bracing beams either." (19)

Question: How does this actual make-up of the floor design relate to Thomas Eager's 'zipper theory' which was mentioned earlier?

Witness 10: "Eager's zipper scenario is impossible given the cross-trussing." (19)

Question: Is there any other reason why the truss theory doesn't hold up?

Witness 10: "There had to have been strong connections between the perimeter wall and the central core so that the wind load on the towers could be transmitted to the central core." (23) "Thus, there must have been strong steel girders connecting the perimeter wall to the central core, not merely trusses." (23)

Question: Which means?

Witness 10: "These girders would not have suffered catastrophic failure as a result of the impact or the fires." (23)

Question: In your opinion, then, what does the government's truss theory constitute?

Witness 10: "The truss failure theory is just a diversion to avoid the glaring deficiencies of the column failure theory." (19)

Question: Can the truss theory adequately explain the WTC's total annihilation?

Witness 10: "It doesn't begin to explain total collapse." (19)

Question: A previous witness testified that even if all the floors had collapsed, the core would still be standing. Is this accurate?

Witness 10: "The domino-effect collapse of the floor diaphragms would have left both the perimeter wall and the cores standing – the floors would have slid down the cores like records on a spindle." (19)

Question: What we're getting at, then, is that the WTC towers were not flimsy constructions, but were instead very strong. Is this a fair assessment?

Witness 10: "The cores were extremely robust structures. They had 47 box columns each a yard wide, fabricated of steel four inches thick near their bases. Plus, they were abundantly cross-braced and anchored directly into the bedrock." (19)

Question: And did they need the floors to support them?

Witness 10: "They did not need the floor diaphragms for support." (19)

Question: Can any of the government's theories explain the total collapse of these towers?

Witness 10: "None of the official theories can explain total collapses of any kind." (19)

Question: Why?

Witness 10: "Take a close look at the manner in which the towers collapse straight down. For these buildings to collapse in this fashion, <u>ALL</u> of the load bearing supports on the ground floor would have had to fail at <u>exactly the same time</u>." (6)

Question: Could this happen by chance as a result of the fires?

Witness 10: No. "The claim that the collapse was the result of a fire requires the fire to be equally distributed throughout the entire floor of the building, providing equal heat for an equal amount of time, so that all the load bearing members would fail at the exact same time." (6)

Question: Please elaborate.

Witness 10: "Even if somehow the fires could have been as hot as Bazant and Zhou would like for their column failure theory, they still could not level the towers, because the towers had 287 columns which would all have to be weakened to the point of collapse at the same instant to cause the vertical telescoping that we saw in the North Tower, or even the South Tower." (19)

Question: Which brings us back once again to a concept we touched upon earlier. Does asymmetric damage produce symmetric results?

Witness 10: "Asymmetric damage doesn't produce such a symmetric result." (19)

Question: Why?

Witness 10: "Some of the columns would get hotter before others and the tower would topple; it wouldn't collapse into itself." (19)

Question: FEMA wants us to believe that the floors were held to the columns in only two places. Is this accurate?

Witness 10: No. "The floors were grids of steel." (41)

Question: And it would have taken more than one or two bolts to 'pop out' for a collapse?

Witness 10: "In order for the floor to fall, hundreds of joints had to break almost simultaneously on 236 exterior columns and 47 core columns. FEMA does not bother to explain how this could occur." (41)

Question: Lastly, let's return to the 'heated and deformed' bolts which the NOVA special says led to the falling floors. Did heat from the fires melt the steel, causing the joints to fail?

Witness 10: No, because "all the joints between the platter and the central columns would have to be heated at the same rate in order to collapse at the same time – and at the same rate as the joints with the outer rim columns on all sides." (4)

Question: And if they weren't all heated at the same rate and at the same time?

Witness 10: "One side of the platter would fall, damaging the floor below and making obvious distortions in the skin of the building, or throwing the top of the tower off balance and to one side." (4)

Question: Would there have been enough heat trapped inside the building to melt all of these hundreds and thousands of bolts at the same time?

Witness 10: No.

Question: Why not?

Witness 10: "Windows ran to the top of the full ceiling – thus the heat accumulation would have been relatively negligible, given the open ventilation from the volume of broken windows – evidenced by the wind carrying the smoke away." (16)

Question: Plus, as we have heard in earlier testimony, the fires were not significantly spreading to other floors. What does this mean in regard to the truss-collapse theory?

Witness 10: "The heat could <u>not</u> have been universally distributed over an entire single floor, let alone over ten floors." (16) "Thus, it's ludicrous to believe that the heat uniquely accumulated, versus ventilated, so as to disastrously diminish the strength of industrial steel in such a short period of time." (16)

WITNESS ELEVEN

Steel Tests and Steel Building Fires

Question: We have been hearing testimony from previous witnesses in regard to the strength of the WTC towers that refutes the government's version of events. What can you tell us about the strength of steel buildings?

Witness 11: Jerry Russell, Ph. D., said in *Proof of a Controlled Demolition at the WTC*: "Steel frame towers are built very strong. They need to withstand the pressure of gale-force winds, the violent rocking motion of earthquakes, and the ravages of time. For this reason, they are <u>almost impossible to destroy</u>." (7)

Question: Can fire bring down a steel-framed building?

Witness 11: "Never in the history of steel-framed structures has a single one been destroyed by fire." (7)

Question: Have tests ever been performed to verify this opinion?

Witness 11: "In the mid-1990s British Steel and the Building Research Establishment performed a series of six experiments at Cardington to investigate the behavior of steel frame buildings. These experiments were conducted in a simulated, eight-story building. Secondary steel beams were not protected." (1)

Question: And what did they find?

Witness 11: "Despite the temperature of the steel beams reaching 1,500-1,700 degrees Fahrenheit in three of the tests – well above the traditionally assumed critical temperature of 1100 degrees F – <u>no collapse</u> was observed in any of the six experiments." (1)

Question: As we've shown in previous testimony, temperatures at the WTC never reached anywhere near that critical point, did they?

Witness 11: No they did not.

Question: In the Cardington tests and in real-life fires like the one at Broadgate, were the beams sprayed with fire-retardant material?

Witness 11: "After the Broadgate Phase 8 fire and the Cardington frame tests there were benchmarks to test composite frame models. Research intensified because almost all the tests had unprotected steel beams." (28)

Question: Which means?

Witness 11: There were "no fire-rated suspended ceilings and no spray-on fire retardant." (28)

Question: And did the buildings fall even though they weren't protected?

Witness 11: "Collapse was not seen." (28)

Question: Have there been any similar tests on steel structures?

Witness 11: Yes. "Corus Construction Company performed extensive tests in multiple countries in which they subjected steel-framed car-parks, which were uninsulated, to prolonged hydrocarbon fueled fires." (19)

Question: A hydrocarbon fire being one similar to that created by jet fuel?

Witness 11: Correct.

Question: And what did they find?

Witness 11: "The highest temperatures they recorded in any of the steel beams or columns were a mere 680 degrees Fahrenheit." (6)

Question: How did these temperatures affect the steel?

Witness 11: "At that temperature, structural steel loses only about 1% of its strength." (6)

Question: What about at higher temperatures?

Witness 11: "Structural steel at 1,022 degrees F still has 60% of the strength of steel at normal temperatures." (24)

Question: In earlier testimony we learned that many support structures need, by law, to be capable of holding three-times the maximum weight that should ever be applied to them. For the WTC towers, that ratio was actually 5:1. What does this specifically mean?

Witness 11: "If a bridge is rated to carry one ton, it should be capable of bearing five tons without collapse." (24)

Question: What do these figures mean in regard to the WTC towers and their maximum load ratios?

Witness 11: "Going back to the fire at the WTC, we can see that reducing the steel structure to 60% of its rated strength should <u>not</u> have weakened it to catastrophic collapse." (24)

Question: Why?

Witness 11: "Because at 60% it would still support three-times the rated load." (24)

Question: And how far would the steel have had to have been reduced?

Witness 11: "The steel structure would have to be reduced to 20% of its rated strength to collapse." (24)

Question: So, even if the temperatures reached 1,022 degrees F, which, by the way, they did not reach, the towers would have still stood?

Witness 11: "Even if the fire had heated the steel to 1,022 degrees F, it would not have been sufficient to cause the towers to collapse." (24)

Question: You mentioned a moment ago that for collapse to occur, steel would have to be reduced to 20% of its rated strength. What is that exact temperature?

Witness 11: "The Corus page on fire vs. steel supports shows that the steel would have to be heated to about 1,320 degrees F to weaken the steel to 20% of its cool strength." (24)

Question: We seem to have two very important temperatures being related to us. Please explain the significance of 1,022 degrees F and 1,320 degrees F.

Witness 11: At 1,022 degrees F, steel "loses elasticity and becomes plastic." (24)

Question: Which means?

Witness 11: "Elasticity means that when the steel is bent, it returns to its original shape; it springs back. Plasticity means that the steel is permanently deformed and does not spring back to the original shape." (24)

Question: 1,320 degrees F is an even more important temperature. Why?

Witness 11: Because at that temperature, it "would be weakened to 20% of its original strength." (24)

Question: And at this temperature the steel would lose enough strength to begin the collapse process?

Witness 11: Correct.

Question: Very well. Now, returning to the Corus fire tests, I understand they set a number of automobiles on fire in steel, multi-storied car-parks. What did these autos contain?

Witness 11: "The parked vehicles were loaded with gasoline, diesel, tires, engine oil, engine tar, upholstery, and hydraulic fluid, etc." (24)

Question: Anything else?

Witness 11: "Any number of cars could contain almost any household item from shopping." (24)

Question: How would you compare these items to that which was inside the WTC?

Witness 11: "These materials are similar to the materials we would expect in the burning offices of the WTC." (24)

Question: What about the fuel used in the automobiles?

Witness 11: "Jet fuel, which is refined kerosene, is very similar to the diesel used in some European cars." (24)

Question: Where were the experiments performed?

Witness 11: In England, Japan, Australia, and the United States. (24)

Question: Was the steel used in these car-park tests better protected or less protected than that in the WTC towers?

Witness 11: "None of the steel was protected with the thermal insulation that is commonly used in office buildings, including the WTC." (24)

Question: Thus, it would be inferior?

Witness 11: Correct.

Question: What was the end result of these tests?

Witness 11: "The maximum temperature reached in the actual test fires in open-sided car-parks in four countries was 680 degrees F." (24)

Question: How did these relatively low temperatures affect the untreated steel?

Witness 11: "The structural steel had sufficient inherent resistance to withstand the effects of any fires that were likely to occur." (24)

Question: Were there any limits on how long these test fires burned for?

Witness 11: No. It "does not limit the duration of the fire." (24)

Question: What precisely does that mean?

Witness 11: "It does not appear to matter whether the fire burned all week or just for two hours. No mention is made – as some people have suggested from erroneous interpretation of other graphs involving time – that prolonged heat brings about progressive weakening of steel." (24)

Question: So what can we conclude from these tests?

Witness 11: "To my mind, this is a definitive answer: the maximum temperature in the unprotected steel supports in those test fires was 680 degrees Fahrenheit, and that is a long way from the first critical threshold in structural steel, 1,022 degrees F." (24)

Question: Wasn't there more fuel involved in the WTC fires?

Witness 11: Yes, but "there was also much more steel involved, the support columns were much more massive, and they were protected with insulation." (24)

Question: What do these tests ultimately tell us?

Witness 11: "Fire did not weaken the WTC structure sufficiently to cause the collapse of the towers." (24)

Question: Okay, let's change our focus. How long have steel buildings been in use?

Witness 11: "Steel-frame high-rises have been in use for over a century." (19)

Question: And to repeat, have any of them ever collapsed due to fire?

Witness 11: "No steel-frame high-rise has ever collapsed due to fire." (19)

Question: Have any of these structures ever caught on fire during the past 100 years?

Witness 11: Yes.

Question: Please provide an example.

Witness 11: "In 1991 fires at One Meridian Plaza in Philadelphia burned for 18 hours and gutted 8 floors of the 38-story building." (45)

Question: How would you describe this fire?

Witness 11: "Uncontrolled." (28)

Question: Are there other examples of steel building fires?

Witness 11: Yes. "In 1988 the First Interstate Bank building in Los Angeles burned out-of-control for 3½ hours, gutting four of the tower's 62 floors." (45)

Question: What characteristics would you give to each of these fires?

Witness 11: "Both fires exhibited large emergent flames, extensive window breakage, and blazes filling multiple, entire floors." (19)

Question: What was the result of each fire?

Witness 11: "All the steel columns and beams at One Meridian Plaza remained intact. The building was subsequently refurbished." (45)

Question: And for the First Interstate Bank building in Los Angeles?

Witness 11: "Afterward, a company that analyzes the causes and effects of building fires, Iklim Ltd., reported: In spite of the total burnout of four and a half floors, there was no damage to the main structural members and only minor damage to one secondary beam and a small number of floor pans." (45)

Question: Please compare these two fires to the WTC towers in regard to the time and ferociousness of the flames.

Witness 11:

- One Meridian Plaza – 18 hour duration – uncontrolled fires

- First Interstate Bank – 4.5 hour duration – uncontrolled fires

- WTC 1 (North Tower) – 1 hour 43 minute duration – minor fires

- WTC 2 (South Tower) – 56 minute duration – minor fires

Question: How would you describe these fires to those in the WTC towers?

Witness 11: "The fires in these two skyscrapers were more severe than those in the three steel-framed World Trade Center buildings that totally collapsed." (45) "These fires were much worse than those in the Twin Towers and Building 7." (19)

Question: Despite their much greater intensity and duration, were the Meridian/Interstate steel columns damaged?

Witness 11: "Neither fire significantly damaged the vertical steel columns." (19)

Question: Did the One Meridian Plaza building, which raged for 18 hours, collapse?

Witness 11: "It did not come close to bringing down the building." (42)

Question: Likewise, describe the First Interstate fire, and also tell us if it collapsed?

Witness 11: "The First Interstate Bank fire in Los Angeles showed greater heating effects over larger regions than those observed in either tower, rained broken window glass down on the streets below, and presented a considerable hazard to those on the ground. The First Interstate Bank did not collapse." (28)

Question: Could the fires in either WTC tower be described as raging out of control?

Witness 11: No.

Question: If they were raging out of control, what would we have seen?

Witness 11: "The steel would glow red-hot, there would be extensive window breakage, bright emergent flames would be visible, and light smoke, not the black smoke that we saw, at least as time progressed, would have been evident." (19)

Question: And if we recall from earlier testimony, when the second plane hit the South Tower, the North Tower was already emitting black smoke and few flames after only 16½ minutes. And the South Tower was an even smaller fire. Do you find this scenario peculiar?

Witness 11: "The fire in the South Tower seems insignificant in comparison to both the Meridian Plaza fire and the fire in the North Tower. How could the tiny fire in the South Tower cause the entire structure to shatter into dust after fifty-six minutes while much more extreme fires did not cause the Meridian Plaza building to even crack into two pieces?" (43)

Question: To what do we contribute the lack of collapse in steel buildings?

Witness 11: "Fires would have never caused a column failure in any steel structure because steel has a high thermal conductivity, which means you pour heat onto it, and it soaks away – the heat conducts very rapidly." (19)

Question: What does this mean in regard to the WTC towers?

Witness 11: "The jet fuel fire did not heat the concrete slabs or the fire-protected steel appreciably. Large columns such as the core columns would also not heat appreciably, even if they had lost their fire-protection. Unprotected trusses may have experienced a more sizeable temperature increase. But the jet fuel fire was so brief that the concrete and steel simply could not absorb the heat fast enough, and consequently, most of the heat was lost to the atmosphere through the smoke plume." (28)

Question: And once the jet fuel fire was over?

Witness 11: "After the jet fuel fire was over; burning desks, books, plastic and carpets contributed to the fire." (28)

Question: Which made this fire become what?

Witness 11: "Now we had a typical office fire." (28)

Question: Would this office fire have made the trusses collapse?

Witness 11: "The fact that the trusses received some advanced heating will be of little consequence. After some minutes the fire would have been indistinguishable from a typical office fire, and we know that the truss-slab combination will survive such fires, because they did so in the 1975 WTC fire." (28)

Question: Lastly, how did FEMA weigh-in on the uncontrolled 18-hour fire at One Meridian Plaza in 1991?

Witness 11: "FEMA's 1991 report describes it as such: After the fire, there was evident significant structural damage to horizontal steel members and floor sections of most of the fire damaged floors. Beams and girders sagged and twisted – some as much as three feet – under severe fire exposures, and fissures developed in the reinforced concrete floor assemblies in many places." (41)

Question: What was their final conclusion?

Witness 11: "Despite this extraordinary exposure, the columns continued to support their loads without obvious damage." (41)

WITNESS TWELVE
Exploding Pulverized Concrete

Question: How much concrete was used in the two World Trade Center towers?

Witness 12: "425,000 cubic yards." (38)

Question: And after each tower fell to the ground in Manhattan, what did witnesses describe regarding this concrete?

Witness 12: "Dr. Robert Schuller was on television telling about his trip to the ruins. He announced in the interview that there was not a single block of concrete in that rubble. From the original 425,000 cubic yards of concrete that went into the buildings, all was dust." (4)

Question: Were there any other reports?

Witness 12: "*The History Channel* spoke with Colonel John O'Dowd of the U.S. Army Corps of Engineers. O'Dowd, who is no stranger to disaster scenes, said that he never saw anything like what he saw at the site where the towers once stood: At the World Trade Center sites, he said, it was like everything was pulverized. Other than the miles of twisted steel beams and columns, there was nothing recognizable in the debris pile – nothing to indicate that the pulverized debris had been, just seconds earlier, a functioning 10,000,000 square foot office building." (34)

Question: How about photographic evidence?

Witness 12: "Photos of the rubble only show a few small pieces of concrete, which means that virtually every piece of concrete shattered into dust. As a result, perhaps 100,000 tons of concrete in each tower was pulverized to a powder." (46) "Every photo of the rubble shows that nothing but steel remained. How can buildings fall down without at least some of the office furniture, plumbing fixtures, and concrete surviving? How is such annihilation possible?" (41)

Question: What other descriptions were there?

Witness 12: "The steel structure was shredded. It was as if the buildings were put through some giant shredding machine. The perimeter wall was chopped into small pieces. The core structures were virtually obliterated, leaving no pieces more than about 30 feet long." (19) "All that was left at the base of the towers was piles of twisted metal. Virtually all of the non-metallic components and contents of the building were converted to fine, sub-100-micron powder. Nearly all the office contents were pulverized beyond recognition, and over 1000 bodies could not be identified even after a year of painstaking analysis with the most advanced DNA techniques because they had been, according to the medical examiner, vaporized." (19)

Question: Does this seem peculiar to you?

Witness 12: Yes, because "it takes hours to cremate a body with temperatures over 500 degrees Fahrenheit." (19)

Question: And how about the area around the WTC complex?

Witness 12: "By the end of the day the area around the World Trade Center was covered with concrete and gypsum powder up to several inches thick." (41) "The dust was deposited around Manhattan in tremendous quantities – up to four inches thick at distances of 2,300 feet from the collapse site." (6)

Question: Where did this thick layer of dust come from?

Witness 12: "Most of the concrete, drywall, and fireproofing in the buildings ended up as dust." (6)

Question: What was this phenomenon reminiscent of?

Witness 12: It looked "as if a volcano had erupted nearby." (41)

Question: To your knowledge, did any volcanoes erupt on the morning of 9-11 in New York City?

Witness 12: No they did not.

Question: Why is this information about microscopic concrete dust important to know?

Witness 12: "The significance of the thick coating of powder becomes more apparent when you look at the collapses, burnings, and bombings of other buildings. When has a building produced such large volumes of powder? This was not a typical collapse." (41)

Question: Did this powder derive from burnt office supplies and equipment?

Witness 12: No. "The streets of New York were full of powdered concrete and gypsum, not ash from burned office materials." (41)

Question: Does concrete typically turn into a fine dust?

Witness 12: "No concrete that I have ever known pulverized like that. It is unnerving. My experience with concrete has shown that it will crumble under stress, but rarely does it just give up the ghost and turn to powder." (4)

Question: What are you saying, then, about every concrete floor, from the first story to the 110th?

Witness 12: "Every concrete floor disintegrated into tiny particles before it hit the ground." (41)

Question: What would happen if we dropped a cinder block from the top of the WTC towers to the street below?

Witness 12: "A block of concrete dropped from a height of 1360 feet would shatter into small pieces, but would not be reduced to microscopic particles." (45)(18) Also, David Ray Griffin quotes Eric Hufschmid in *The New Pearl Harbor*: Even concrete slabs hitting the ground at free-fall speed would not be pulverized." (46)

Question: Then how could this phenomenon occur?

Witness 12: "In order to pulverize concrete into powder, explosives must be used." (41)

Question: Please tell us more about this possible use of explosives."

Witness 12: "When the towers started to collapse, they did not fall straight down as the pancake theory holds. They exploded. The powder was ejected horizontally from the buildings with such force that the buildings were surrounded by enormous dust clouds that were perhaps three times the width of the buildings themselves." (46)

Question: And you attribute this to the use of explosives?

Witness 12: "What other than explosives could turn concrete into powder and then eject it horizontally 150 feet or more." (46) "Why didn't the pieces simply fall down? Why were they ejected with such force?" (41)

Question: Was anything else ejected from the towers?

Witness 12: "Heavy pieces of steel were ejected in all directions for distances up to 500 feet, while aluminum cladding was blown up to 700 feet away from the towers." (45)

Question: That's nearly two football fields for the heavy steel, and over two football fields for the external aluminum casing.

Witness 12: Correct. There's even "a gash in World Financial Center 3, about 400 feet away from the North Tower, and it's several hundred feet up." (19)

Question: Was the concrete dust also ejected outward?

Witness 12: Yes. "Thick dust clouds spewed from the towers in all directions at about 50 feet/second." (19)

Question: That's roughly about 34 miles/hour, is it not?

Witness 12: Correct.

Question: What else can you tell us about the concrete dust being thrown from the towers?

Witness 12: "Each of these mushrooming tops remained centered around the towers' vertical axes, and they expanded to about three-times each tower's diameter in five seconds, and about five-times their diameter in ten seconds." (19)

Question: As for the objects being propelled outward, along with the dust; which was thrust out ahead of the other?

Witness 12: "Solid objects were thrown ahead of the dust." (18)

Question: What is this indicative of?

Witness 12: This is a "feature of explosive demolition." (18)

Question: And what about the few pieces of steel that were inspected by FEMA. What was found?

Witness 12: "The steel was thoroughly cleansed of its spray-on insulation." (18)

Question: Can any of these anomalies be attributed to, or caused by, fire?

Witness 12: "Fire did not and could not have caused the Twin Towers, or any other building's concrete, to spontaneously explode into a fine powder, nor could fire have caused steel beams to be broken and propelled hundreds of feet horizontally." (9)

Question: Could fire have been the energy source for this dramatic transformation of concrete to powder?

Witness 12: "Concrete does not turn to powder very easily, even if it is roasted in fire." (41)

Question: Is there any way that an everyday person could test this for themselves?

Witness 12: Yes, build a house out of your child's Lincoln Logs, then collapse it by pulling one or two pieces out. See if any of the wooden logs are thrust violently out across the room. (41)

Question: In your opinion, then, did the towers simply fall down?

Witness 12: "As anyone can plainly see from any photos and/or videos of the destruction of the World Trade Center, the Twin Towers did not fall apart and fall down. They each exploded in a progressive wave from their upper floors and near the impact zones downward toward their basements." (9)

Question: For clarity, explain what happened as the buildings descended toward the ground.

Witness 12: While "they collapsed completely and vertically," (9) at the same time "the fractured steel and other solid debris was propelled, at high speeds, horizontally, hundreds of feet in all directions." (9)

Question: So the building was falling downward while huge explosions were being created horizontally?

Witness 12: Correct.

Question: Did these huge eruptions of concrete dust begin immediately as the towers began to collapse?

Witness 12: Yes. "When the upper portion of the North Tower fell down onto the base [the intact portion below it], it fell a distance of only one or two floors." (41)

Question: Would it be traveling very quickly?

Witness 12: "It would not be traveling very fast when it hit the base." (41)

Question: Why is that?

Witness 12: Because "it should at most be accelerating under gravity at 32 feet per second." (22)

Question: So, in simplest terms, it wouldn't have built up a head of steam?

Witness 12: No. "It is very hard to imagine a physical mechanism generating that much dust with concrete slabs bumping into each other at 20 or 30 mph." (22)

Question: But even at this very early juncture, are there huge clouds of concrete dust being ejected?

Witness 12: "You can see thick clouds of pulverized concrete being ejected within the first two seconds. That's when the relative motion of the top of the tower to the intact portion was only a few feet per second." (19) "Dust begins to appear in quantity in the very earliest stages of the collapses, when nothing else is moving fast relative to anything else in the structure." (22)

Question: Was the energy possessed by this falling 'cap' within the first second or two enough to pulverize concrete?

Witness 12: "Within the first few seconds of the collapses, the motion of the falling top relative to the intact structure was only a few feet per second. Clearly the speed of the falling top relative to the building was insufficient to convert concrete to fine powder." (41)

Question: After the first floor fell only a few feet, what would we expect to happen?

Witness 12: "It might crack the floors, bend some steel beams, and even bust a few holes in the flooring; but how could it shatter into dust after falling such a short distance?" (41)

Question: Could this dust actually be smoke from the burning fire?

Witness 12: No.

Question: Why not?

Witness 12: "Prior to the collapse only small wisps of black smoke were seeping from the tower and rising upward. But when the top section began to tip, enormous clouds were expelled horizontally out of the tower, all around the crash zone. These clouds were not the smoke of a fire. Rather, something was occurring inside the tower to create large amounts of powder, and then expel that powder at high velocity.... How could the powder be ejected with such a high velocity that the clouds reached perhaps 200 to 400 feet wide?" (41)

Question: To reiterate, how fast do things happen at the onset of a gravity fall?

Witness 12: "During the first few seconds of a gravitational fall, nothing is moving very fast." (22)

Question: Could the dust clouds be attributed to burning jet fuel combined with gravity?

Witness 12: "The energy required to heat this huge mass sufficiently to reduce it to powder is very difficult to account for by any reasonable combination of gravitational and combustion effects, without the input of additional energy from explosives." (6)

Question: So you're telling us that it would have taken an enormous amount of energy to transform concrete into powder?

Witness 12: "Cracking a concrete block into two pieces requires energy, and converting a concrete block into powder requires even more energy. The smaller the particles, the more energy needed." (41)

Question: And how much concrete in each tower was turned to dust?

Witness 12: "Perhaps 100,000 tons of concrete in each tower was pulverized into powder. This required a lot of energy. Plus, the powder was ejected with a velocity so high that clouds of dust expanded to two or three-times the diameter of the building. This also required energy. Thousands of steel beams in the building broke at their joints, and breaking these joints required energy. Energy was also needed to shred the corrugated steel sheets that were part of every floor. The high temperature of the rubble required energy as well." (41)

Question: Does accounting for the extremely powerful energy source become problematic?

Witness 12: "The biggest and most obvious problem that I see is the source of the enormous amount of very fine dust that we see generated during the collapse. Where does the energy come from to turn all this reinforced concrete into dust?" (46)

Question: What if someone didn't believe that explosives were used. What would you tell them?

Witness 12: "I suspect that many of the people who refuse to believe explosives were used have never tried to bust a concrete slab. Most people seem to believe that concrete has about the same strength as chalk." (41)

Question: But if it were this delicate?

Witness 12: "It would not be safe to use it in bridges." (41)

Question: What if someone used a jackhammer to break concrete? Would it turn to powder?

Witness 12: "Breaking concrete into pieces is a common procedure around the world. Pneumatic jackhammers are designed specifically for this purpose. But jackhammers do not pulverize concrete into powder; rather, all they do is crack it into pieces." (41)

Question: Is any powder created while doing so?

Witness 12: "Only a small amount of powder is created in the process." (41)

Question: What would it take to turn concrete into a fine dust?

Witness 12: "In order to pulverize concrete into powder, explosives must be used. Concrete will not turn into powder simply by falling down onto another piece of concrete." (41)

Question: I hate to be redundant, but can gravity alone accomplish this feat?

Witness 12: "It is simply impossible to create and disperse this amount of material using only the energy of a gravitational collapse, yet it is seen being ejected from the earliest moments of the collapses." (22)

Question: Were the floors at the onset moving very quickly?

Witness 12: "At this point the floors are moving at tens of miles per hour and provide no mechanism for grinding all that concrete into fine dust." (22)

Question: "What would it take then?

Witness 12: "Without the use of high explosives, such a rapid and complete pulverization is very difficult indeed to explain." (22)

Question: Strangely, the concrete was pulverized in mid-air, even before it hit the ground. Is this correct?

Witness 12: Jim Marrs wrote in *Inside Job*: "Nearly all the concrete was pulverized in the air, so finely that it blanketed parts of lower Manhattan with inches of dust. In a gravity collapse, according to Jim Hoffman, there would not have been enough energy to pulverize the concrete until it hit the ground, if then." (44)

Question: Did it take a force much greater than gravity to pulverize the concrete, which acted upon it before even hitting the ground?

Witness 12: "Independent scientists cited by Hoffman in a highly technical paper have shown that the energy required for the pulverization of this much concrete and for the stupendous expansion of the dust clouds is as much as 100 times greater than could have been produced from each tower's gravitational potential energy (i.e. mass times height)." (44)

Question: Does this also apply to the solid objects thrown outward at least 500 feet?

Witness 12: Yes. Again, Jim Marrs quotes Jim Hoffman: "The downward forces of a gravity collapse cannot account for the energetic lateral ejection of pieces." (44)

Question: Plus, as we will hear from our next witness, these towers fell at nearly the rate of free-fall. How would this affect the pulverization of concrete?

Witness 12: "These astounding rates of fall, according to Hoffman's technical explanation, indicate that nearly all resistance to the downward acceleration of the tops had been eliminated ahead of them." (44)

Question: So the buildings were falling through the air with no resistance – a virtual gravity free-fall – yet they're EXPLODING outward at the same time! Is this correct?

Witness 12: Yes. "Remember that the towers fell at almost the speed of a gravitational free-fall, meaning that little energy was expended doing anything other than accelerating the floor slabs." (22)

Question: And this means?

Witness 12: "This means very little of the gravitational energy can have gone toward pulverizing the concrete." (22)

Question: Lastly, when we examine photos of these dust explosions, we see that some of the clouds are dark in color, while others are light. Why?

Witness 12: "The upper clouds are mixed with black smoke from the fire, while the lower clouds are pure concrete, gypsum, and whatever else has been pulverized." (41)

Question: Which means?

Witness 12: "The white clouds show that the pulverization process is occurring in that portion of the tower below the fire zone." (41)

Question: The part which wasn't even on fire?

Witness 12: Yes. "This was the area of the tower that was cool, so the steel and concrete in that area were still at their maximum strength." (41)

Question: Yet a pulverization process was still taking place where absolutely no damage had occurred?

Witness 12: Yes. "The structure shattered anyway." (41)

WITNESS THIRTEEN
Gravity Free-Fall

Question: How quickly did the WTC towers fall to the ground?

Witness 13: "The Twin Towers each fell at roughly the rate of free fall." (9)

Question: Which means?

Witness 13: "They each fell at about the same speed that an object would if it were dropped from the roof." (9)

Question: And how long did this take?

Witness 13: Depending on precisely what one defines as the complete fall of each tower, the average is approximately 10-13 seconds.

Question: Why this discrepancy? Why can't we arrive at an exact time?

Witness 13: Due to the overwhelming amount of concrete dust that smothered the towers, it is difficult to tell precisely when the roof of each building touched the ground. A time of 10.4 seconds has been bandied about quite a bit as an average, but we'll settle for anywhere from 10-13 seconds.

Question: Fair enough. While the buildings were falling, what was also happening at the same time?

Witness 13: "Debris is being blown away from the buildings with an extremely powerful blast." (42)

Question: If there was absolutely no resistance whatsoever acting upon these towers, how long would it have taken them to fall to the ground?

Witness 13: "An object in a vacuum would take 9.2 seconds to fall from the towers' height." (36)

Question: Is there a formula we can use to calculate and verify this figure?

Witness 13: Yes. "The time (t) required for an object to fall from a height (h) in a vacuum is given by the formula: t=square root (2h/g), where (g) is the acceleration due to gravity (32.174 feet/second squared)." (20)

Question: Please run us through this calculation.

Witness 13: Okay. The average height of the two towers is 1,365 feet (1,368 and 1,362). So, if we double that we arrive at 2,730. Now, if we divide that number by the acceleration due to gravity – 32.174 – we arrive at 84.85. Finally, the square root of 84.85 equals 9.211, or rounded-off, 9.2 seconds.

Question: So, let's get this straight. If the towers collapsed in a no-resistance, gravity free-fall, it would take them 9.2 seconds to reach the ground?

Witness 13: Correct.

Question: And on the morning of 9-11, 2001, they took only 10-13 seconds to actually fall?

Witness 13: Correct.

Question: So the difference between a gravity free-fall and the actual descent time is only 1-3 seconds?

Witness 13: Correct.

Question: If it had taken each floor only one second to fall upon the one below it, what would have been the total elapsed collapse time?

Witness 13: Since each tower was 110 stories high, approximately 110 seconds.

Question: Which is nearly ten times longer than the actual collapse time?

Witness 13: Correct.

Question: And for the towers to collapse, what would have had to happen?

Witness 13: In regard to the South Tower, "following the start of the collapse the upper floors would have had to shatter the steel joints in all 85 or so floors at the lower levels." (20) "In order for a floor to fall, hundreds of joints had to break almost simultaneously on 236 columns and 47 core columns." (41)

Question: Very well. Now, let's return to the collapse time of each tower. From what we've determined, there appears to be very little resistance acting upon these massive structures. Is that correct?

Witness 13: Yes.

Question: But should there have been resistance?

Witness 13: Of course.

Question: And what would have provided this resistance?

Witness 13: The Twin Towers were 110 stories high, and combined they contained 200,000 tons of steel, 425,000 cubic yards of concrete, and each tower weighed 500,000 tons. (38)

Question: How many pounds is 500,000 tons equivalent to?

Witness 13: One billion pounds.

Question: Should a combined mass of one billion pounds provide resistance?

Witness 13: It should provide an enormous amount of resistance!

Question: Is there anything else that should have provided resistance beyond the billion pounds of this structure itself?

Witness 13: Every floor of these 110 story structures was nearly an acre in size. And each of these floors undoubtedly held hundreds of computers, desks, cabinets, chairs, and other furniture. All of these items would have provided tons of resistance to a falling body.

Question: But what did we find in regards to resistance?

Witness 13: "In just ten seconds, 10,000,000 feet of commercial office space simply ceased to exist." (35) "It was as if the entire building was falling straight down through the air. As if the entire solid structure, below the strong part which had not been burned or sliced or harmed in any significant way, just disappeared into nothingness." (7)

Question: In your opinion, what is this reminiscent of?

Witness 13: "This, within a small tolerance, is what we would expect to find if there had been a controlled demolition." (7)

Question: Why did you form this conclusion?

Witness 13: "Because the explosions below left the upper stories completely unsupported." (7)

Question: Should that part of the building below the impact points have provided resistance?

Witness 13: Yes. "Gravitational acceleration cannot achieve its full effect if it is fighting any opposing force. In the case of the World Trade Center, the intact building below should have at least braked the fall of the upper stories." (7)

Question: Did this happen?

Witness 13: "This did not happen. There was no measurable friction at all." (7) "The only way a building can fall at free-fall speed is for there to be no resistance at all." (22)

Question: Does the reality of this situation adhere to the laws of science, specifically the laws of falling bodies that was postulated by Galileo?

Witness 13: No. "This defies the laws of gravity!" (42)

Question: Why?

Witness 13: Because "there was resistance, and plenty of it. The resistance was the massive lower sections of the buildings that were stabilized by over 250 major interior and exterior steel columns, and thousands of steel trusses!" (42)

Question: Could there be a problem with the scientific formulas being used in our calculations?

Witness 13: "Either the height of the buildings is inaccurate, the time of the falls is inaccurate, the scientific calculation that has been used for hundreds of years is inaccurate, or ... something pulled down those buildings at a faster rate." (42)

Question: Okay, from videotape footage and from earlier testimony we know that objects from within the towers were ejected outside the buildings as they collapsed. Did these falling objects encounter more, less, or the same amount of resistance as that of the falling towers?

Witness 13: "Rubble falling through the towers encountered no more resistance than rubble falling through the air." (10)

Question: Does this scenario seem peculiar to you?

Witness 13: Eric Hufschmid asks this question about objects inside the WTC towers: "How could debris crush 100 steel and concrete floors while falling as fast as objects falling through the air?" (41)

Question: What does this mean?

Witness 13: "You have stuff that's falling freely through the air outside the profile of the building and stuff that's falling through where the building was -- it's all falling at the same speed." (19)

Question: What was providing resistance to those objects falling outside the building?

Witness 13: "Air resistance was the only thing slowing the descent of the rubble outside the footprint." (36)

Question: And of course, what should have provided resistance inside the towers?

Witness 13: "1,000 vertical feet of intact vertical structure would have been slowing the rubble inside the footprint, barring demolition." (36)

Question: But what do we find in terms of resistance inside and outside of the towers?

Witness 13: "Air resistance slowed the descent of the rubble outside the building's profile by about 50% compared to the rate of free-fall in a vacuum. But the over 1,000 vertical feet of intact structure did not slow portions falling within the profile any more than air." (45)

Question: How do we know this?

Witness 13: "This can be verified by examining the top of the North Tower's dust cloud, which is essentially the same height both inside and outside the building's profile." (45)

Question: Which ultimately means?

Witness 13: "If air could slow down the fall of debris from 9.2 seconds to 14 seconds, say a 50% slowdown in the rate of fall because of air friction, how much more should the huge intact structures -- the thousand foot vertical structure of these buildings -- how much more should that have slowed down the fall of the rubble within the profile of the building? A hundred times? A thousand times? And yet it falls at about the same rate." (19)

Question: Which you interpret as?

Witness 13: "Clearly, again, the building was being demolished ahead of the falling rubble." (19) "They fell as though there were no floors below the collapsing section to 'pancake' onto, as though there was no resistance to the progressive collapse but air." (9)

Question: How is this possible?

Witness 13: "The only way this is possible is if the floors were destroyed progressively before the mass above them could meet their resistance." (9)

Question: Did the floors above ever touch the ones below them?

Witness 13: "Each floor was shattered <u>before</u> the debris above it was about to make contact." (41)

Question: Which means?

Witness 13: "The end result is that the debris <u>never collided with the floors</u>. Rather, all debris was in free-fall." (41)

Question: Again, how is this possible?

Witness 13: "This is possible only if all structural support had been completely eliminated prior to the initiation of the collapse. Since the lower floors were undamaged by the plane impacts and the fires, the removal of all structural support in these floors must have been due to some other cause." (20) "Since a steel structure should have provided hundreds, if not thousands of times the resistance of air, it must have been demolished <u>ahead of the falling mass</u>." (36)

Question: What, then, can we conclude?

Witness 13: "The towers fell in roughly ten seconds. That is, they fell at about the same rate that an object falls through air. The fact that the towers fell this quickly – essentially at the rate of free-fall – is conclusive evidence that they were deliberately demolished." (5)

Question: This is a bitter pill for many people to swallow. What would you say to them?

Witness 13: "Believing that there is nothing wrong with the towers collapsing so quickly is roughly analogous to believing that people pass through closed doors as quickly as they pass through open ones. The fact that they fell at such a rate means that they encountered essentially no resistance from the supposedly undamaged parts of the structure. That is, no resistance was encountered from any of the immensely strong parts of the structure that held the building up for the last 30 years. This just doesn't happen, unless, of course, the lower part of the building has lost its structural integrity." (5)

Question: How would a building lose its structural integrity?

Witness 13: "This is usually due to the detonation of a multitude of small explosive charges as seen in controlled demolitions." (5)

Question: And how, precisely, was this accomplished?

Witness 13: "A few floors shattered during the first second, but that rate of disintegration did not hold steady. Rather, the number of floors shattering each second increased each and every second. The reason is that objects falling in gravity continuously increase in speed, so the explosives were detonated at an increasingly faster rate in order to stay ahead of the falling objects." (41)

Question: And this is ultimately why the lower sections provided no resistance to the upper portions?

Witness 13: Yes. "(a) The top section of the tower did not collide with the base; rather, the explosives shattered it just before it would have made contact. (b) The debris did not contact the base portion; rather, the explosives were always staying a few microseconds ahead of it. (c) The overhanging section cannot be seen falling down in photographs in one large chunk because it was shattered by explosives. Its debris fell down at the rate objects fall in gravity, but none of the debris can be seen in photographs because the base was always a few microseconds ahead of the debris." (41)

Question: Finally, did the concrete dust create a smokescreen of sorts for this entire process?

Witness 13: Somewhat. "The steel beams fell much faster than the dust, so the steel beams were actually passing through the clouds of dust. However, new clouds were created at the same rate at which the debris was falling. Therefore, as soon as a steel beam fell below one particular cloud, it entered a new cloud that had just been created a few microseconds earlier. By the time it fell below that cloud, another cloud had been created below it. The end result was that all of the falling objects were always hidden by clouds of dust." (41)

WITNESS FOURTEEN
Eyewitness Testimony

Question: There's been quite a bit of testimony thus far in this trial about a controlled demolition bringing down the WTC towers. Is there any evidence of this from eyewitnesses who were directly on the scene?

Witness 14: Yes. I'll break them down into four categories: reporters, employees, firemen, and others in an official capacity.

Pat Dawson – an NBC Correspondent who filed this report on the morning of 9-11: "The Chief of Safety of the Fire Department of New York told me that, uhh, he thinks that there were actually devices that were planted in the building. One of the secondary devices he thinks that took place after the initial impact was, he thinks, may have been on the plane that crashed into one of the towers. The second device, he thinks, he speculates, was probably planted in the building. Uhh, so that's what we've been told by, uhh, Albert Turi, who is the Chief of Safety for the New York City Fire Department. He told me that just moments ago." (34)

Transcript from Pat Dawson interview – "The Chief of Safety of the Fire Department of New York City told me shortly after 9:00 he had roughly ten alarms, roughly 200 men, trying to effect rescues of some of those civilians who were in there; and that basically he received word of a secondary device, that is another bomb going off. He tried to get his men out as quickly as he could, but he said that there was another explosion which took place. And then an hour after the first hit there, the first crash that took place, he said there was another explosion that took place in one of the towers here. So obviously, according to his theory, he thinks that there were actually devices that were planted in the building." (29)

Steve Evans – BBC reporter who was in the South Tower at the time of the attacks: "I was at the base of the second tower, the second tower that was hit. There was an explosion – I didn't think it was an explosion – but the base of the building shook. I felt it shake ... then when we were outside, the second explosion happened and then there was a series of explosions ... we can only wonder at the kind of damage – the kind of human damage – which was caused by those explosions, those series of explosions." (44)

Fox 5 News New York City – shortly after 10:00 a.m. on September 11, they videotaped a large white cloud of smoke billowing near the base of the South Tower. The commentator exclaimed: "There is an explosion at the base of the building ... white smoke from the bottom ... something has happened at the base of the building ... then, another explosion. Another building in the World Trade Center complex." (44)

WLS Radio Broadcaster in Chicago – a reporter on the scene at the towers "reported that his colleague had witnessed an enormous fireball emanating from beneath one of the towers immediately before it came crashing down." (34)

Teresa Veliz – manager for a software development company – survived after reaching ground level of the North Tower: "The flashlight led us into Borders bookstore, up an escalator and out to Church Street. There were explosions going off everywhere. I was convinced that there were bombs planted all over the place and someone was sitting at a control panel pushing detonator buttons. I was afraid to go down Church Street toward Broadway, but I had to do it. I ended up on Vesey Street. There was another explosion. And another. I didn't know which way to run." (44)

Ross Milanytch – watching from the 22nd floor of a building a couple blocks from the WTC complex: "I saw small explosions on each floor. And after it all cleared, all that was left of the buildings, you could just see the steel girders in like a triangular sail shape." (44)

Auxiliary Fire Lieutenant Paul Isaac Jr. – also mentions bombs when telling reporter Randy Lavello that: "New York firemen were very upset by what they considered a cover-up in the WTC destruction. 'Many other firemen knew there were bombs in the buildings, he said, but they are afraid for their jobs to admit it because the higher-ups forbid discussion of this fact. Isaac, who was stationed at Engine 10 near the WTC in the late 1990s, said the higher-ups included the NYFD's antiterrorism consultant, James Woolsey, a former CIA director. 'There were definitely bombs in those buildings,' Isaac added." (44)

Tom Elliott – Aon Corporation – after descending from the 103rd floor before Flight 175 struck the South Tower (as reported to the *Christian Science Monitor* in an article entitled *A Changed World* – September 17, 2001): "Although its spectacularly televised impact was above Elliott, at first he and those around him thought an explosion had come from below. An incredible sound – he calls it an 'exploding' sound – shook the building, and a tornado of hot air and smoke and ceiling tiles and bits of drywall came flying up the stairwell. In front of me, the wall split from the bottom up, Elliott said." (43)

John O'Neill – head of WTC security – stated shortly before becoming a victim himself that "he had helped dig out survivors on the 27th floor before the building collapsed. Since the aircraft crashed into the 80th floor, what heavily damaged the 27th floor?" (43)

Louie Cacchioli – 51-year-old fireman – Engine 47 Harlem, in *People Weekly*, September 24, 2001 edition: "We were the first ones in the second tower after the planes struck. I was taking firefighters up in the elevator to the 24th floor to get in position to evacuate workers. On the last trip up a bomb went off. We think there were bombs set in the building." (43)(45)

New York City Firemen Discussing the Explosions:

Fireman 1: Floor by floor it started popping out ...

Fireman 2: It was almost like they had detonators ...

Fireman 3: Yeah, detonators ...

Fireman 2: ... planted to take the building down. Boom-boom-boom-boom-boom ...

Fireman 1: All the way down. I was watching it and running. (5)

Mike Pecoraro – Stationary Engineer, North Tower 6th sub-basement: "Climbing to Level C of the basement, Pecoraro found a machine shop and its 50-ton hydraulic press both 'gone,' reduced to rubble, he told *Chief Engineer* magazine. He saw a 'line of smoke streaming through the air' on Level C. He climbed to Level B, one floor below the North Tower's lobby, and saw 'a steel and concrete fire door that weighed about 300 pounds.' He described this door as wrinkled up 'like a piece of aluminum foil.'" (45)

Paul Biggert – photographer: "What you are seeing in his photos are large numbers of twelve-foot sections of perimeter columns flying out ahead of the dust cloud in what is very clearly an explosive event. He [Biggert] got very close to the North Tower just before it fell, and captured some amazing pictures of its collapse and of the previous damage from the WTC 2 collapse. What is clear, especially in Biggert's picture, is that the building is turning to dust as, or even before, it falls." (5)

David Handschuh: "Instinctively I lifted a camera up, and something took over that probably saved my life. And that was to run rather than take pictures. I got down to the end of the block and turned the corner when a wave – a hot, solid, black wave of heat threw me down the block. It literally picked me up off my feet, and I wound up about a block away." NOTE: "What this witness is describing is known as a 'shockwave effect.' When an explosion goes off, extremely high temperatures are generated in a small amount of time and space. This abrupt shift in temperature causes the air to push outwards with violent force, seeking to stabilize itself." (5)

Joe Casaliggi – Engine 7 fireman – in the documentary *911* by Jules and Gedeon Naudet: "Casaliggi told the filmmakers how he was one of the workers assigned to look for survivors, and while he foraged through the wreckage, he found that everything, including chairs, electronic equipment, desks, and even the telephones had been utterly pulverized to dust." Transcript from the movie: "You have two 110-story office buildings. You don't find a chair, you don't find a telephone, a computer ... the biggest piece of a telephone I found was half a keypad, and it was this big (holds up thumb and forefinger). The buildings collapsed to dust." (47)

Phillip Morelli – construction work – to *NY1 News* – "When the North Tower was struck he was thrust to the ground by two explosions in the fourth sub-basement. Somewhat later, another explosion (which made the walls explode) once again hurled him to the ground. Morelli then exited that building and went inside the South Tower's sub-basement, where once again he felt the same type of underground explosions." (47)

Larry Klein – producer of *Why the Towers Fell* – recounting the wreckage that he witnessed: "There was not a discernable piece of furniture anywhere. No computers or books or anything that would identify this massive wreckage field as having once been several million square feet of office space ... I didn't need anyone to tell me that the gray-brown matter was the contents and insides of the World Trade Center vaporized by the collapse." (47)

WITNESS FIFTEEN
Seismographic Data

Question: We have thus far heard extensive testimony from various witnesses and experts speaking about controlled demolitions and bombs being set off inside the World Trade Center towers. Is there any other physical evidence to corroborate this testimony?

Witness 15: Yes, seismographic data.

Question: Where was this data recorded?

Witness 15: "At Columbia University's Lamont-Doherty Earth Observatory." (5)

Question: Where is this facility located?

Witness 15: "In Palisades, New York, 21 miles north of the WTC." (5)

Question: What does the data from this facility show?

Witness 15: "The Palisades seismic record shows that – as the collapses began – a huge seismic 'spike' marked the moment the greatest energy went into the ground." (15)

Question: When precisely did this happen?

Witness 15: "The Palisades seismic data recorded a 2.1 magnitude earthquake during the ten-second collapse of the South Tower at 9:59:04, and a 2.3 quake during the eight-second collapse of the North Tower at 10:28:31." (15)

Question: And when did these jolts occur?

Witness 15: "The strongest jolts were all registered at the beginning of the collapses, well before the falling debris struck the earth." (15)

Question: Are you saying that the most profound seismic activity took place before crashing debris struck the ground?

Witness 15: Yes. "The energy source that shook the ground beneath the towers was many times more powerful than the potential energy released by the falling mass of the towers." (15)

Question: To what do you attribute this?

Witness 15: According to Dr. Arthur Lerner-Lam, Director of Columbia University's Center for Hazards and Risk Research, as quoted in *Earth Institute News*: "Most of the energy of the falling debris was absorbed by the towers and the neighboring structures, converting them into rubble and dust or causing other damage – but <u>not causing</u> significant ground shaking." (20)   Lerner-Lam also added: "The groundshaking that resulted from the collapse of the towers was extremely small." (5)

Question: Did the impact of each jetliner hitting the towers cause any seismic activity?

Witness 15: "While the aircraft crashes caused minimal earth shaking, significant earthquakes with unusual spikes occurred at the beginning of each collapse." (15)

Question: How do these spikes that occurred at the <u>beginning</u> of each collapse compare to the spikes created when the towers actually hit the ground?

Witness 15: "The two unexplained spikes are more than twenty times the amplitude of the other seismic waves associated with the collapses." (15)

Question: Again, when did these spikes occur?

Witness 15: "As the buildings <u>began</u> to fall." (15)

Question: What do these powerful initial bursts – that occurred as the towers began to fall – indicate?

Witness 15: Quoting Arthur Lerner-Lam: "A ten-fold increase in wave amplitude indicates a 100-fold increase in energy released." (15)

Question: Could you put this concept into some type of perspective for us?

Witness 15: Seismologist Won-Young Kim told the *American Free Press* that, "The Palisades seismographs register daily underground explosions from a quarry 20 miles away. These blasts are caused by 80,000 pounds of ammonium nitrate and cause local earthquakes between magnitude 1 and 2." (15)

Question: So the seismic data on the morning of 9-11 that occurred as the towers began to fall and before they reached the ground was 2.1 for the South Tower and 2.3 for the North Tower?

Witness 15: Correct.

Question: And this is equivalent to or greater than the force created by 80,000 pounds of underground ammonium nitrate explosions from a quarry 20 miles away?

Witness 15: Correct.

Question: Considering this testimony, what does this seismic activity tell you?

Witness 15: "These unexplained 'spikes' in the seismic data lend credence to the theory that massive explosions at the base of the towers caused the collapses." (15)

Question: And you can determine this from the seismic data?

Witness 15: David Ray Griffin writes in *The New Pearl Harbor* in regard to author and researcher Eric Hufschmid: "The shocks increased during the first five seconds, then dropped abruptly to a lower level for about three seconds, and then slowly tapered off. This pattern, Hufschmid suggests, reflects the fact that the first explosives detonated were those near the tops of the towers where the steel columns were the thinnest. The shocks got stronger as the detonation pattern, controlled by a computer program, worked its way down. The final explosions at the base of the tower and in the basement had to break joints on columns made from 100 mm thick steel [3.93 inches thick], so they were powerful explosives." (46)

Question: And this is when we see the most volatile seismic activity?

Witness 15: "The seismic data peaked when the explosives in the basement were detonated. Then the explosives stopped and the rubble continued to fall for another couple of seconds, resulting in small seismic tremors." (46)

Question: Such a scenario may sound ludicrous to some people. How would you respond to their misgivings?

Witness 15: Mark Loizeaux, president of Controlled Demolition, Inc, who was responsible for the WTC clean-up, was asked if the vertical support columns gave way before the connections between the floors and columns. He responded, "If I were to bring the towers down, I would put explosives in the basement to get the weight of the building to help collapse the structure." (15)

Question: Would you characterize Loizeaux as an expert in his field?

Witness 15: Yes, as president of Controlled Demolition, Inc, who refer to themselves as "the innovator and global leader in the controlled demolition and implosion of structures." (15)

WITNESS SIXTEEN
Molten Steel

Question: After the World Trade Center towers collapsed, what did rescue workers initially find at Ground Zero?

Witness 16: The *American Free Press* reported that "pools of molten steel were found at the base of the collapsed twin towers weeks after the collapse." (15)

Question: Where specifically did this information originate?

Witness 16: From "Mark Loizeaux, president of Controlled Demolition, Inc, who arrived on the WTC site two days later and wrote the clean-up plan for the entire operation." (15)

Question: And he confirmed the pools of molten steel?

Witness 16: "*AFP* asked Loizeaux about the report of molten steel on the site. 'Yes' he said, 'hot spots of molten steel in the basements'." (15)

Question: Where precisely were these pools found?

Witness 16: "At the bottoms of the elevator shafts of the main towers, down seven basement levels, Loizeaux said." (15) "The molten metal could be found at the bottom of the debris, as opposed to being melted over or among the debris." (16)

Question: And how long was it there?

Witness 16: "Three, four, and five weeks later, when the rubble was being removed, Loizeaux said." (15)

Question: Was this molten steel found anywhere else?

Witness 16: Loizeaux said, "Molten steel was also found at WTC 7." (15)

Question: Before moving on, tell us about the foundations of these towers.

Witness 16: "The foundations were 70 feet deep at that level. 47 huge box columns, connected to the bedrock, supported the entire gravity load of the structures." (5)

Question: How thick was the steel used in these box columns?

Witness 16: "The steel walls of these lower box columns were four inches thick." (5)

Question: Has anyone else confirmed the existence of this molten steel?

Witness 16: Yes.   "Peter Tully, president of Tully Construction of Flushing, New York, told the *American Free Press* of 'literally molten steel' at the World Trade Center." (15)

Question: How far below street level was this molten steel?

Witness 16: "70 feet below the surface." (15)

Question: Since it was seven stories below street level, were these pools of molten steel covered by rubble from the collapsed towers?

Witness 16: Yes.

Question: How would you describe the environment surrounding this molten steel?

Witness 16: It was "an oxygen starved environment." (15)

Question: Is an oxygen starved environment conducive to the perpetuation of burning substances?

Witness 16: Obviously it is not.

Question: Why is that?

Witness 16: According to the National Interagency Fire Center: "Fuel, heat and oxygen are all needed in the right combination to produce fire." (3)

Question: If any of these components are eliminated, what happens?

Witness 16: "Take away any of the three components of fire – fuel, heat or oxygen – and the fire collapses, meaning that it can't burn." (3)

Question: Yet this molten steel in an oxygen starved environment continued to boil for up to five weeks?

Witness 16: Correct.

Question: An earlier witness testified that a temperature of 5,182 degrees Fahrenheit is required to transform steel into a liquefied molten state. Is this correct?

Witness 16: It is.

Question: Another witness testified that the highest temperature that could have possibly been attained inside the WTC towers after the initial fireball was 680 degrees Fahrenheit?" Is that correct?

Witness 16: It is.

Question: Finally, a third witness testified that 16½ minutes after the North Tower was struck, it was already a dwindling, oxygen starved fire which was not spreading to other areas of the tower, while the South Tower was an even smaller, very containable office fire. Are these assessments correct?

Witness 16: They are.

Question: And what is the variance in temperatures between the proposed fire temperature inside the towers and that required to turn steel into molten steel?

Witness 16: 5,182 degrees minus 680 degrees equals a variance of 4,502 degrees.

Question: Yet how long after 9-11 was this molten substance found burning beneath the fallen towers?

Witness 16: "Hot spots of literally molten steel were discovered more than a month after the collapse." (15) "Intense heat persisted in the bottoms of the rubble piles for months. The fires continued to burn for 100 days, despite being sprayed with water." (19)

Question: A previous witness testified that jet fuel from the crashing airliners burned-off within 1-2 minutes. Is this accurate?

Witness 16: It is.

Question: Could fire from the burning jet fuel that was extinguished in 1-2 minutes have created temperatures of 5,182 degrees Fahrenheit?

Witness 16: They "could not possibly have been produced by residual hydrocarbon fires." (19)

Question: What would you need to produce molten steel?

Witness 16: "Normally you need a blast furnace to achieve that kind of heat." (19)

Question: To your knowledge, were there any blast furnaces seven stories beneath the streets of Manhattan?

Witness 16: No, there were not.

Question: Has anyone from the government been able to explain this seemingly inexplicable phenomenon?

Witness 16: "The energy source for these incredibly hot areas has yet to be explained." (15)

Question: A previous witness spoke about strange seismic data that occurred precisely when the towers began collapsing. In your opinion, could this testimony be related to the pools of molten steel?

Witness 16: "Two unexplained 'spikes' in the seismic record from September 11 indicate huge bursts of energy shook the ground beneath the World Trade Center towers immediately prior to the collapse." (15)

Question: Which means?

Witness 16: "These spikes suggest that massive underground explosions may have literally knocked the towers off their foundations, causing them to collapse." (15)

Question: A previous witness testified that only a very small percentage of the WTC steel wreckage was actually inspected. Is this correct?

Witness 16: "Only a tiny fraction of all steel beams in the World Trade Center were inspected." (41)

Question: Of those pieces that were inspected, what was discovered?

Witness 16: "A few of them were very peculiar. A *New York Times* article in February, 2002 declared: pieces of steel have also been found that were apparently melted and vaporized not solely because of the heat of the fires, but also because of a corrosive contaminant that was somehow released in the conflagrations." (41)

Question: In your opinion, would it take a temperature higher than 5,182 degrees Fahrenheit – the molten steel threshold – to vaporize steel?

Witness 16: Definitely so.

Question: Did *The New York Times* article that you previously mentioned arrive at any conclusions about this bizarre occurrence?

Witness 16: Yes. They wrote, "The steel apparently melted away, but no fire in any of the buildings was believed to be hot enough to melt steel outright." (41)

Question: Is there any other way we could confirm the existence of these 'hot spots'?

Witness 16: Yes. "On September 16, five days after the attacks, NASA flew a plane over the site to take measurements." (42)

Question: Before they took these measurements, what steps were taken at Ground Zero?

Witness 16: "In this period of time hundreds of truckloads of debris had already been carried off, and firemen had sprayed millions of gallons of water on the smoking rubble." (42)

Question: What did NASA use to take their measurements?

Witness 16: "NASA used an Airborne Visible/Infared Image Spectrometer (AVIRIS) to locate and measure the site's hot spots." (15)

Question: What did NASA find?

Witness 16: "The results show that there were several 'hot spots' with temperatures over 1000 degrees F on the surface, with one spot at the South Tower that recorded 1,377 degrees!" (42)

Question: How did this 1,377 degree surface temperature compare to the molten steel?

Witness 16: It was "less than half as hot as the molten steel in the basement." (15)

Question: How are these dramatically high temperatures explained?

Witness 16: "The one unexplained WTC issue is the continuing fire from below the collapsed debris." (16)

Question: Could it have been caused by burning jet fuel?

Witness 16: "This was <u>NOT</u> jet fuel." (16)

Question: How do we know that?

Witness 16: "By virtue of the smoke color. Any residual liquid fuel would have been burned or dispersed – essentially evaporated – on the way down." (16) "Jet fuel, burning in open air, will reach roughly 1,100 degrees – insufficient to actually melt steel. Certainly it can weaken steel, but not melt it down. The WTC jet fuel did not burn in open air, thus a lower temperature may reasonably be assumed." (16)

Question: Could these extreme temperatures have been caused by the weight of falling debris?

Witness 16: "Since neither tons of jet fuel, nor a compression demolition have the potential to create this type of heat – much less maintaining this heat for days afterwards – an impartial detective would have to conclude that there was another source for these extreme temperatures!" (42)

Question: Are there any other reasons why the falling debris could not have created these drastic temperatures?

Witness 16: "An argument for 'mechanical energy transmission' doesn't hold up." (16)

Question: Why?

Witness 16: "It's not the same as hitting a nail with a sledgehammer. A 'shattering' sledgehammer would not carry the force to strike, deform, and 'heat' a nail." (16)

Question: So when you hit a nail with a sledgehammer – which is comparable to the tower's collapse – the hammer doesn't melt or vaporize the nail, or turn it to molten steel?

Witness 16: Correct. "The force of the collapse couldn't / didn't melt the bases of the core columns." (16)

Question: So the hammer could bend a nail or drive it into something, but nothing beyond that?

Witness 16: "Bending steel with horrendous energy is one thing, melting it is another." (16)

WITNESS SEVENTEEN

Controlled Demolition

Question: The words 'controlled demolition' have been mentioned quite frequently during this trial by various witnesses and the sources they've quoted. Are you aware of any other instances when individuals 'in the know' have referred to the WTC collapse as a controlled demolition?

Witness 17: Yes. "In *New Scientist* magazine, Mike Taylor of the National Association of Demolition Contractors in Doylestown, PA said that the collapse of the WTC towers looked like a classic controlled demolition." (26) In the same edition of this magazine (September 12, 2001), the following quote appeared: "The collapse of the WTC towers mirrored the strategy used by demolition experts. In controlled demolitions, explosives are placed not just on the lowest three floors, but also on several consecutive floors about a third of the way up the building." (26)

Question: Are these arguments supported by other professionals?

Witness 17: "The controlled demolition theory is given additional support by the fact that some people, including some firemen, reported hearing explosions, feeling explosions, or witnessing effects that appeared to be results of explosions, both in the intermediate floors and in the sub-basements of the towers." (46)

Question: Were there any others who have stepped forward right after 9-11 to voice this opinion?"

Witness 17: Yes, Van Romero.

Question: Who is he?

Witness 17: "Romero is vice president of research at the New Mexico Institute of Mining and Technology, which studies explosive materials and the effects of explosions on buildings, aircraft, and other structures, and often assists in forensic investigations into terrorist attacks, often by setting off similar explosions and studying the effects." (27) He is also "an explosives expert and former director of Energetic Materials and Testing Center at New Mexico Tech." (27)

Question: What did this gentleman say specifically about the WTC collapse?

Witness 17: Romero told the *Albuquerque Journal* on September 11, 2001: "My opinion, based on videotapes, is that after the airplanes hit the World Trade Center there were some explosive devices inside the buildings that caused the towers to collapse." (35)

Question: In your opinion, if anyone would know about such matters, would it be Romero?

Witness 17: Yes.

Question: What else did he tell the *Albuquerque Journal*?

Witness 17: He said, "The collapse of the structures resembled the controlled implosions used to demolish old structures and was too methodical to be a chance result of airplanes colliding with the structures." (27) He also added that, "It would be difficult for something from the plane to trigger an event like that. It could have been a relatively small amount of explosives placed in strategic points." (35)

Question: Did Romero say why such a technique was used?

Witness 17: "One of the things terrorist events are noted for is a <u>diversionary attack</u> and <u>secondary device</u>, Romero said. Attackers detonate an initial, diversionary explosion, in this case the collision of the planes into the towers, which brings emergency personnel to the scene, then detonate a second explosion." (27)

Question: In this light, I'd like to return to the collapse of each tower. In earlier testimony we learned that it should have been impossible for the South Tower to fall first, yet it did. Why?

Witness 17: "The North Tower was hit by an airplane first, and its fires were the most severe. So why did the South Tower collapse first? My guess is: the collapses were supposed to appear realistic. This required the towers to collapse while the fires were burning. However, the fires in the South Tower were so small and there were so many firemen rushing in that there was a risk that the fires would soon become insignificant. It would look suspicious if the fires vanished and <u>then</u> the tower crumbled." (41)

Question: Since we're on the subject, do controlled demolitions, especially in two of the tallest structures on earth, require a significant amount of time and planning?

Witness 17: Yes. "A considerable amount of study, planning and preparation is required." (35) "Demolishing a building is not something you can do in a few minutes by tossing explosives into a basement. It actually takes days of planning." (5)

Question: Why is that?

Witness 17: Because "specific quantities of explosives have to be precisely placed at key structural locations throughout the building, and those explosive charges have to be programmed to detonate in a specific pattern." (35) "You have to pinpoint all the load-bearing structures, then you have to wire everything and set the cutting charges so they all go off in a predestined order." (5)

Question: With controlled demolitions, is there a lot of room for error?

Witness 17: "There is almost no margin for error." (35)

Question: So this isn't something that could hastily be done on a moment's notice?

Witness 17: Definitely not.

Question: Are there a great number of companies who are equipped to engage in such undertakings?

Witness 17: "Only a handful of companies have the technical expertise to take on such a project." (35)

Question: How, then, in simplest terms, is a controlled demolition executed?

Witness 17: "The explosives are detonated simultaneously, destroying the integrity of the steel frame at key points, such that no part of the building is supported against the force of gravity." (7)

Question: What happens then?

Witness 17: "The entire mass is pulled swiftly to earth, where gravity does the work of pounding the structure into tiny fragments of steel and concrete." (7)

Question: What science is involved in this process?

Witness 17: "The gravitational potential energy of the structure is converted smoothly and uniformly into kinetic energy, and then is available very efficiently to pulverize the fragments of the building as they impact against the unyielding earth." (7) "In a controlled demolition, gravity does the lion's share of the work, while the explosives serve only to destroy the physical integrity of the structure." (30)

Question: If successful, what is the overall appearance of a controlled demolition?

Witness 17: "Controlled demolitions have the striking and characteristic appearance of a smooth, flowing collapse." (7)

Question: With all this testimony pointing toward a controlled demolition, why didn't FEMA likewise point to this possibility?

Witness 17: "FEMA had been given an impossible assignment – to explain the collapse of this building while remaining within the framework of the official theory." (46)

Question: Why?

Witness 17: "Not being able to suggest that the collapse resulted from a controlled demolition, the best FEMA could come up with was a theory only having a low possibility." (46)

Question: Does this apply to others who advanced the 'official' theory?

Witness 17: "The same understanding must be applied to Thomas Eager and all the other experts who have presented highly improbable explanations of the collapse of the Twin Towers." (46)

Question: Are you saying their hands were tied?

Witness 17: "If political correctness were not a factor so that they could simply state the most probable hypothesis, given the evidence, most of them would surely choose controlled demolition." (46)

Question: Are you saying they obfuscated information to keep it from leading toward a controlled demolition?

Witness 17: "FEMA's report hides and minimizes the core structures whose existence made the symmetric total collapses of the towers due to gravity impossible." (45)

Question: And how much space did FEMA give to these vitally important core structures?

Witness 17: "Destroying the core columns is key to achieving total building collapse. And yet FEMA's report has only one short passage explaining how the cores self-destructed." (45)

Question: If the North tower was struck at 8:46 a.m., would a demolition company be able to rush in and successfully wire it by the time it fell 102 minutes later?

Witness 17: Not a chance.

Question: Likewise, could a demolition company successfully wire the South Tower to fall in the 56 minutes between when it was struck and when it fell?

Witness 17: Again, not a chance.

Question: So, if the World Trade Center towers were wired for a controlled demolition, when would it have had to have been done?

Witness 17: "This demolition was planned long before 9-11!" (5)

Addendum

Ten characteristics that are standard features of "controlled demolition" collapses, which are produced by explosives placed throughout a building and set to go off in a particular order. (From <u>David Ray Griffin's book</u> – *The 9/11 Commission Report: Omissions and Distortions*. (48)

1. Each collapse occurred at virtually free-fall speed.

2. Each building collapsed straight down, for the most part into its own footprint.

3. Virtually all the concrete was turned into very fine dust.

4. In the case of the Twin Towers, the dust was blown out horizontally for 200 feet or more.

5. The collapses were *total*, leaving no steel columns sticking up hundreds of feet into the air.

6. Videos of the collapses reveal "demolition waves," meaning "confluent rows of small explosions."

7. Most of the steel beams and columns came down in sections that were no more than 30 feet long.

8. According to many witnesses, explosions occurred within the buildings.

9. Each collapse was associated with detectable seismic vibrations (suggestive of underground explosions).

10. Each collapse produced molten steel (which would be produced by explosives), resulting in "hot spots" that remained for months.

9/1/07

WITNESS EIGHTEEN
WTC 7

Question: One of the most neglected aspects of 9-11 was the collapse of World Trade Center Building No. 7. As our final witness, give us a brief overview of what happened.

Witness 18: "At 3:00 p.m., photos of Building 7 show a few small fires on two floors." (41) "CNN and other news agencies have a timeline of events on September 11, and they report Building 7 on fire at 4:10 p.m." (41) "At 5:20 p.m., Building 7 collapses." (41)

Question: How far away from the Twin Towers was WTC 7?

Witness 18: "Building 7 was 355 feet away from the North Tower, and still farther from the South Tower." (46)

Question: What is the 'official' reason given by the government for WTC 7's collapse?

Witness 18: According to the FEMA report: "Debris from the collapse of the World Trade Centers also initiated fires in surrounding buildings, including WTC 4, 5, 6, and 7; 90 West Street; and 130 Cedar Street. Many of the buildings suffered severe fire damage but remained standing. However, two steel-framed structures experienced fire-induced collapse. WTC 7 collapsed completely after burning unchecked for approximately seven hours." (37)

Question: If the first reports of fire in WTC 7 were at 3:00 p.m., and it fell at 5:20 p.m., how much elapsed time is that?

Witness 18: Two hours and twenty minutes.

Question: In your opinion, is there a great deal of discrepancy between 7 hours and 2 hours and 20 minutes?

Witness 18: There is.

Question: How does FEMA say WTC 7 fell?

Witness 18: "Studies of WTC 7 indicate that the collapse began in the lower stories, either through failure of major load transfer members located above an electrical substation structure or in columns in the stories above the transfer station." (37)

Question: Before we get to the actual collapse of this building, let's examine FEMA's claim that the WTC 7 fire burned unchecked for seven hours.   Is this statement truthful?

Witness 18: No. "The fire in Building 7 was supposedly so extreme that it caused a steel building to crumble. However, all photos show only a few tiny fires in only a few windows, and only tiny amounts of smoke were produced." (41)

Question: What do you make of this dramatic discrepancy in the FEMA report?

Witness 18: "I would think that a fire of the magnitude necessary to collapse a steel building would have set fire to a lot of the office furniture, carpeting, and other flammable objects." (41)

Question: What would this have done?

Witness 18: "This in turn would have caused a lot of flames to be visible in a lot of windows. Also, I suspect that such a large fire would have caused many windows to shatter." (41)

Question: Does the photographic evidence show this?

Witness 18: No. "How could an incredible fire burn in the building without any photos showing evidence of large flames or tremendous plumes of smoke?" (41) "There is no evidence of any raging fire.   Every photo taken of Building 7, Hufschmid reports, shows only a few tiny fires in only a few windows, primarily on the 7th and 12th floors." (46)

Question: How would you ultimately describe these fires?

Witness 18: "The fires in Building 7 were so small that you could safely roast marshmallows over them." (41)

Question: Has the government produced photos of a raging inferno at WTC 7?

Witness 18: "Still photos or video footage of WTC 7 engulfed in flames are curiously hard to find." (35)

Question: How about right before its collapse?

Witness 18: "Photos of the building taken not long before the collapse reveal only small pockets of fire that were confined to two floors." (35)

Question: Did the FEMA report contain photos of WTC 7; and if so, what did they show?

Witness 18: "The FEMA report contains photos of Building 7 that were taken shortly after the collapse of the North Tower." (41)

Question: This would have been approximately 10:30 a.m.?

Witness 18: Yes.

Question: And what do these photos show?

Witness 18: "The photographs show a small amount of damage to the exterior of Building 7 as a result of flying debris." (41)

Question: And the fires only broke out at about 3:00 p.m.; is that correct?

Witness 18: Yes. "FEMA has no idea how this small amount of damage started fires inside the building." (41)

Question: We've learned from previous testimony that never before in the history of the world has a steel building collapsed due to fire. But at least with the Twin Towers there was the added element of jetliners crashing into them. Did aircraft of any kind strike WTC 7 on the morning of 9-11?

Witness 18: No.

Question: What can we derive from this fact?

Witness 18: "The collapse could not be partly explained by the impact and fuel of an airplane, so WTC 7 would be the first steel-framed building in history to collapse solely from fire damage." (46)

Question: Yet the fires were so small as to be insignificant. Is that correct?

Witness 18: Yes.

Question: Should this anomaly be important to people?

Witness 18: "This would be an event of overwhelming importance." (46)

Question: Why?

Witness 18: "Everything that architects and building engineers have long assumed about steel-framed buildings would need to be rethought. Insurance companies around the world would need to recalculate all their rates on the basis of the realization that ordinary fires could cause steel-framed buildings to collapse." (46)

Question: Yet how does the government view this outrageously inexplicable situation?

Witness 18: "The idea that WTC 7 collapsed due to fire has been accepted as if it were nothing unusual." (46)

Question: How so?

Witness 18: "In an essay entitled *WTC 7: the Improbable Collapse*, Scott Loughrey says: 'FEMA's nonchalance about WTC 7's collapse is stunning. Structural failures of this magnitude do not normally take place. Do we now live in an era when tall steel buildings can collapse in large cities without any significant discussion why?'" (46)

Question: Some people may not even be concerned with this building, but did WTC 7 have any special significance?

Witness 18: Yes. "Housed on the 23rd floor of the building was Mayor Giuliani's Office of Emergency Management." (34)

Question: Which was?

Witness 18: "A state-of-the-art command center designed to serve as a base of operations during times of crisis." (34)

Question: Was this command post manned on the morning of 9-11?

Witness 18: "The command center was monitoring the situation in lower Manhattan – at least until ..." (34)

Question: Until what?

Witness 18: "Until the personnel staffing the center received an order to evacuate." (34)

Question: Who ordered this evacuation?

Witness 18: "One of the officials manning the command center that day told filmmakers from *The History Channel* that, to this day, we don't know who gave that order." (34)

Question: Okay, if this building had been raging on fire for seven hours as FEMA claims, where were the firemen?

Witness 18: "The fire chief decided, for some unknown reason, not to have his crew enter this building." (46)

Question: Can we confirm this?

Witness 18: Yes. "Tom Franklin, the photographer who took the famous 'Iwo Jima flag-raising' photo on September 11th, was near Building 7 at about 4:00 p.m. In his description of how that photograph came about, he makes an interesting remark about Building 7: Firemen evacuated the area as they prepared for the collapse of Building Seven." (41)

Question: What do you gather from this comment?

Witness 18: "Franklin's remarks show that somebody told the firemen by about 4 to 5 p.m. to stay away from Building 7 because it was going to collapse." (41)

Question: Do you find this odd, especially since all evidence points to the fact that only small fires were burning inside this structure?

Witness 18: "What evidence could anybody have that Building 7 would collapse? Considering that no fire had ever caused the collapse of a steel building before, why would anybody believe Building 7 would crumble from a few tiny fires? Who were those people who told the firemen to stay away?" (41)

Question: Is there any other evidence that firemen were deliberately pulled from what appeared to have been a very minor, manageable fire?

Witness 18: "In September 2002, PBS aired a documentary about construction at the World Trade Center complex that was entitled *America Rebuilds*." (45)

Question: Who or what was featured in this documentary?

Witness 18: "In this one-hour documentary Larry Silverstein [owner of the WTC complex] spoke about tumultuous events on 9/11/01." (45)

Question: What specifically did he say about WTC 7?

Witness 18: "Larry Silverstein said: 'I remember getting a call from the, er, fire department commander, telling me that they were not sure they were gonna be able to contain the fire, and I said, we've had such terrible loss of life, maybe the smartest thing to do is pull it. And they made that decision to pull and we watched the building collapse.' " (45)

Question: Did he mean that they wanted to pull firemen from the scene, or 'pull' the building down, which is a common term for a controlled demolition?

Witness 18: According to Dave McGowan in *9-11 Revisited*: "Many researchers have suggested that Silverstein admitted on public television that he and the FDNY made a joint decision to bring WTC 7 down in a controlled demolition. This is a particularly nasty line of disinformation because it casts the FDNY, universally viewed (and rightfully so) as the heroes of 9-11, as co-conspirators in bringing the buildings down. It is perfectly clear from the context of Silverstein's statement that he was not suggesting that the building be brought down, but rather that fire fighting operations be suspended. The 'terrible loss of life' he referred to was obviously the loss of scores of firefighters in the Twin Tower collapses, and his point was that it wasn't worth putting any more firefighters at risk, particularly in a building that had long since been evacuated. In what parallel universe would a building owner casually suggest to the fire department that his building be brought down in a controlled demolition, as if such a thing can be engineered on the spot? And how exactly would collapsing an intact building save lives?" (35)

Question: In your opinion, then, what do you feel Silverstein meant by this revealing admission?

Witness 18: Again, according to McGowan: "Far from candidly admitting that he had ordered the demolition of WTC 7, what Silverstein was actually doing was lying to explain why no effort was made to control the easily controllable fires that purportedly brought the building crashing down." (35) From my perspective, though, both scenarios – whether it was firemen being pulled or the building being 'pulled down' – are inexplicable.

Question: Why?

Witness 18: "Every photo taken of Building 7 shows only a few tiny fires in only a few windows. The fires appear so insignificant that I would expect the sprinkler system to put them out." (30)

Question: Then this wasn't a catastrophic situation that required the firemen to be pulled, or the building to be demolished?

Witness 18: "The front of Building 7 has some broken windows and other minor damage from falling debris, but the sides and rear of the building have no damage and only a few fires." (41)

Question: Okay, moving on, at 5:20 p.m., WTC 7 collapsed to the ground. Please describe what happened.

Witness 18: "It appears from pictures to be a totally conventional demolition." (42) "It is nearly impossible to watch video footage of the collapse and fail to recognize it for what it is: a deliberate, and perfectly executed, controlled implosion." (35)

Question: How have you reached this conclusion?

Witness 18: "There were no huge explosions, the building walls fell neatly in on themselves, and the rubble was cracked and broken, not pulverized." (42)

Question: Are there any specific characteristics that show signs of a controlled demolition?

Witness 18: Yes. In Don Paul and Jim Hoffman's book, *Waking Up from Our Nightmare: The 9/11/01 Crimes in New York City*, they explain: "This 47-story skyscraper, its height about five times its depth, dropped directly into its footprint in a smooth, vertical motion." (45)

Question: Which means?

Witness 18: "The symmetry of WTC 7's collapse meant that this building's 58 perimeter columns and 25 central columns of structural steel must have all shattered at almost the same instant." (45)

Question: How long did it take this building to fall?

Witness 18: "WTC 7 collapsed completely in less than seven seconds." (45)

Question: Which means?

Witness 18: This was "a time almost equal to that of unimpeded free-fall." (45) "World Trade Center # 7 hit the ground, reduced to a neat pile of rubble in approximately seven seconds. Like the Twin Towers, it was a virtual free-fall." (35)

Question: Please put this in perspective for us.

Witness 18: "If a brick were dropped from 570 feet – the height of Building 7's roof – in a vacuum, it would hit the ground in 5.95 seconds. Thus, the building's falling mass encountered almost <u>no resistance</u>, showing that its structure had been destroyed before the fall." (45)

Question: What other evidence points to a controlled demolition?

Witness 18: "A third telltale feature of demolition is the dust that streamed out of the upper floors of Building 7 early in its collapse." (45)

Question: Why is this strange?

Witness 18: Because "these floors were far removed from the pockets of fire that had been on the building's 7th and 12th floors." (45)

Question: Where do you believe this dust – as opposed to smoke – came from?

Witness 18: "Such streamers are typical artifacts of the numerous small explosive charges used in a controlled demolition." (45)

Question: Can we tell anything from the way this building fell?

Witness 18: Yes. "A fourth sign of demolition is that WTC 7's roof inverted toward its middle as the collapse progressed." (45)

Question: Which means?

Witness 18: "This inversion and the fact that the mechanical penthouse dropped about a second before the façade indicate that the interior structure of the building was destroyed slightly ahead of the perimeter." (45)

Question: Why would this indicate a controlled demolition?

Witness 18: "Controlled demolitions are engineered in this manner to make tall buildings implode." (45)   "When

Building 7 collapsed, the interior fell first, and that caused the outside of the building to move inward, as if the insides were being sucked out. The result was a very tiny pile of rubble, with the outside of the building collapsing on top of the pile. This is how conventional demolitions operate." (41)

Question: Is there a specific reason why?

Witness 18: Yes. "As interior mass falls, it pulls the exterior inward." (45)

Question: Were any of the buildings tightly packed around WTC 7 damaged?

Witness 18: "Only one adjacent building was significantly damaged by the collapse of this huge skyscraper. The two buildings closest to WTC 7, the U.S. Post Office building on the left, and the Verizon building on the right, were barely touched by the collapse." (45)

Question: Earlier testimony showed that the WTC towers smoldered for months after their collapse. Considering the very minor nature of its fire, was WTC 7 extinguished immediately after it fell?

Witness 18: No. "WTC 7's rubble pile continued to smolder for months." (45)

Question: Since I mentioned the Twin Towers, what similarities and differences could be found between their collapse and that of WTC 7?

Witness 18: "The vertical symmetry of the destruction of both Building 7 and the Twin Towers could only have been caused by controlled demolitions. The explosive pattern of destruction in the Towers, however, indicates a far more energetic process was used to destroy them than to destroy Building 7." (45) Also, "Building 7 collapsed at its bottom, causing it to resemble the demolition of an old style building. While a lot of the concrete in Building 7 turned to powder, this building did not break down as thoroughly as the towers." (41)

Question: Do you have any final thoughts on the collapse of WTC 7?

Witness 18: "Building 7 was destroyed later in the afternoon. It was never hit by any airplanes, so there is no known reason – besides explosives – for it to have collapsed into rubble." (7)

Question: And what are FEMA's final thoughts on WTC 7?

Witness 18: FEMA wrote this matter off by commenting: "The specifics of the fires in WTC 7 and how they caused the building to collapse remain unknown at this time." (37)

CLOSING ARGUMENT

In my opening statement, I asked this jury if the truth mattered. I also said that if the search for truth and justice in regard to 9-11 didn't matter to them, what in God's name did? This was undoubtedly the most traumatic event in the history of this nation, and its far-reaching effects still impact us today. Lastly, I added that the preponderance of scientific evidence that we would present would be so overwhelming that the government's "official" version of events would crumble like a house of cards.

Now that you've heard this testimony, I would like to briefly review it:

1) Physical evidence at Ground Zero – a crime scene whose integrity should have been painstakingly preserved – was deliberately and immediately destroyed with blatant disregard.

2) The World Trade Center's extremely strong design was intentionally distorted by "official" sources to make it appear flimsy and weak.

3) FEMA itself revealed that the WTC design was far superior to all structural and fire maximum code requirements.

4) The government's own experts concluded that the impact from two jetliners which struck the Twin Towers was insignificant in toppling them.

5) Mathematical formulas prove that the WTC towers were able to withstand damage from the impact of a Boeing 767.

6) Jet fuel from the crashing airliners completely burned off within 1-2 minutes after impact; the subsequent fires did not spread throughout the towers; and they actually diminished in size over time.

7) There is scientific proof that the maximum temperature of burning jet fuel cannot melt construction grade steel.

8) There is scientific proof that the melting point of construction grade steel is nearly double the maximum temperature of burning jet fuel.

9) FEMA admitted that the towers burned at temperatures well below that of a typical office fire.

10) Firefighter audiotapes prove that the WTC fires were contained and manageable.

11) FEMA admitted that burning jet fuel could not initiate structural damage within the towers.

12) Scientific proof that burning jet fuel could not raise maximum temperatures on the floors where they were burning above 536 degrees F.

13) MIT professor Thomas Eager admitted that steel only collapses after losing 80% of its strength – which can only be reached at 1300 degrees F.

14) Scientific proof that the "wrong" tower inexplicably fell first.

15) Using the laws of physics, we showed the impossibility of how an asymmetric collapse could suddenly become symmetric in a naturally occurring way.

16) Scientific proof that fires nearly three times more intense than those at the WTC were incapable of collapsing steel-framed buildings.

17) 425,000 cubic tons of concrete was pulverized to a fine microscopic dust.

18) Scientific proof that despite collectively weighing a billion pounds, the WTC towers fell in a nearly zero-resistance gravity free-fall.

19) Seismographic data proves that huge spikes were registered before the towers fell, not when they hit the ground.

20) Proof that molten steel still boiled in the WTC sub-basements seven stories below street level five weeks after 9-11 occurred.

Ladies and gentlemen, think about everything that we've learned from this evidence, and how dramatically it differs from the government's "official" version of events. I hope I'm not too brash in saying this, but somebody's lying! And as we've now proven with a substantial amount of evidence – as opposed to theory – it was physically impossible for the World Trade Center towers to collapse the way the government said they did. Why? Because their version of events blatantly violates the laws of science, the laws of physics, the laws of gravity, and the laws of nature. Please understand that we live in a world where these laws cannot be broken.

I'll reiterate this point once again: it was <u>physically impossible</u> for the World Trade Center towers to fall in accordance with the government's "official" version of events. And now we have proven this using scientific formulas, physics, mathematical equations, and expert testimony.

These strong, sturdy, magnificent towers did not simply collapse to the ground due to the impact of two jetliners or the insignificant fires created by them. Instead, they were deliberately destroyed via controlled demolitions that were planned well in advance of 9-11.

Ladies and gentlemen, we have <u>PROOF</u> that the government is lying, and the only "conspiracy theory" now in existence is the one *they're* promoting via their "official" smokescreen version of events. That's the real <u>conspiracy</u> theory, and its time we held the bloodthirsty monsters who were behind it accountable for their vile, traitorous deeds.

The proof is now before us, and those who demolished the Twin Towers are guilty as sin.   Will we allow these evil criminals to keep getting away with what they did, or will we rise en-masse and demand justice?   As you think about this, I'll leave you with a final quote by Edmund Burke: "All that is required for evil to triumph is for good men to do nothing." If we let these monsters get away with the mass-murder that they committed on the morning of 9-11, our silence will be construed as consent, and these madmen will then be capable of doing anything to us in the future. Is that what you want?

REFERENCES

<u>Note</u>: Some of the articles listed below have been ongoing works in progress, so an initial publication date has not been listed, or, where applicable, their initial date of publication is the one listed.

Articles

1. The Jet Fuel: How Hot Did It Heat The World Trade Center?

Vancouver Independent Media Center, February 27, 2003

http://www.vancouver.indymedia.org/news/2003/02/34507.php

2. Why the Towers Fell: Towers Site Map

http://www.pbs.org/wgbh/nova/wtc/dyk.html

3. This Thing Called Fire

National Interagency Fire Center

http://www.nifc.gov/pres_visit/whatisfire.html

4. Muslims Suspend the Laws of Physics

J. McMichael, October 21, 2001

http://www.serendipity.li/wot/mslp_i.htm

5. Evidence of Controlled Demolition

Geronimo Jones, April 24, 2004

http://www.letsroll911.org/articles/controlleddemolition.html

6. Controlled Demolition at WTC: Ongoing Developments – WTC 7

Jerry Russell, Ph. D. & Richard Stanley, March 13, 2004

http://www.911-strike.com/demolition_explosive.htm

7. Proof of a Controlled Demolition at the WTC

Jerry Russell, Ph. D., March 31, 2002

http://www.attackonamerica.net/proofofcontrolleddemolitionatwtc.htm

8. Collapse of the World Trade Center: Engineering Aspects

The University of Sydney: Department of Civil Engineering, September 15, 2001

http://www.freerepublic.com/focus/f-news/524466/posts

9. The Controlled Progressive Collapse of the Twin Towers

Abel Ashes, July 2004

http://suetheterrorists.net/page24.html

10. How Was It Known that the WTC Was Going to Collapse

Colin Bett

http://www.whatreallyhappened.com/wtc_giuliani.html

11. The 9/11 WTC Fires: Where's the Inferno?

Colin Bett

http://www.whatreallyhappened.com/wtc_fire.htm

12. The 9/11 WTC Collapses: An Audio-Video Analysis

Colin Bett

http://www.whatreallyhappened.com/9-11_wtc_videos.html

13. The 'Truss Theory': A Fantasy Concocted to Conceal a Demolition

Colin Bett

http://www.whatreallyhappened.com/trusstheory.html

14. Kevin Ryan Letter to Frank Gayle

Kevin Ryan, November 11, 2004

http://www.thetruthseeker.co.uk/article.asp?ID=2492

15. New Seismic Data Refutes Official Explanation

Christopher Bollyn, American Free Press, September 3, 2002

http://www.americanfreepress.net/09_03_02/NEW_SEISMIC_/ne
w_seismic_html

16. The Mystery of the WTC Collapse

Ralph Omholt, September, 2003

http://home.comcast.net/~skydrifter/collapse.htm

17. Why the Towers Fell – NOVA (PBS)

Produced & Directed by: Garfield Kennedy and Larry Klein,
April 30, 2002

18. The Twin Towers Demolition: Exposing the Fraud of the Government's Story

Jim Hoffman

http://911research.wtc7.net/talks/towers/index.html

19. The Twin Towers Demolition: Text for Slide Presentation

Jim Hoffman, September 11, 2003

http://911research.wtc7.net/talks/towers/text/index.html

20. Evidence for Explosives in the Twin Towers

Peter Meyer, September 13, 2001

http://www.serendipity.li/wtc5.htm

21. Evidence of Explosives in the South WTC Tower Collapse

L.A. Independent Media Organization, December, 2002

http://la.indymedia.org/news/2002/12/23816.php

22. A Discussion of the Physics of the World Trade Center Collapse

Jeff King, September 16, 2002

http://www.plaguepuppy.net/public_html/physics/

23. The World Trade Center Demolition and the So-Called War on Terrorism

Peter Meyer, September 13, 2001

http://www.assassinationscience.com/wtc.html

24. Muslims Suspend the Laws of Physics (part two)

J. McMichael

http://www.serendipity.li/wot/mslp_ii.htm

25. The Split-Second Error: Exposing the WTC Bomb Plot

Fintan Dunne, September 18, 2001

http://www.acts2.com/thebibletruth/PDOWTC.htm

26. Design Choice for Towers Saved Lives

Eugenie Samuel and Damian Carrington

New Scientist Magazine, September 12, 2001

http://www.newscientist.com/news/news.jsp?id=ns99991281

27. Some Survivors Say 'Bombs Exploded Inside WTC'

Christopher Bollyn American Free Press, October 22, 2001

http://www.americanfreepress.net/10_22_01/Some_Survivors_Say_
_Bombs_Expl/some_survivors_say__bombs_expl.html

28. The World Trade Center Demolition

Center for Research on Globalization, March 6, 2004

http://globalresearch.ca.myforums.net/viewtopic.php?t=315

29. 'Explosives Planted in Towers' New Mexico Tech Expert Says

Olivier Uyttebrouck, Albuquerque Journal,

September 11, 2001

http://st12.startlogic.com/~xenonpup//experts/

30. An Analysis of the Energy Needed to Crumble the World Trade Center

Jerry Russell, Ph. D., January, 2002

http://www.erichufschmid.net/WTC_AnalysisRussell.html

31. Thermal Properties and Temperatures

The University of Sheffield

http://www.webelements.com/webelements/elements/text/Fe/heat.html

32. Introduction to the Resistance Welding Process

http://www.publicaction.com/911/jmcm/rwintroduction.html

33. September 11, 2001 Revisited: (part one)

Dave McGowan, September 15, 2004

http://www.davesweb.cnchost.com/nwsltr67.html

34. September 11, 2001 Revisited: (part two)

Dave McGowan, October 2, 2004

http://www.davesweb.cnchost.com/nwsltr68.html

35. September 11, 2001 Revisited: (part three)

Dave McGowan, October 27, 2004

http://www.davesweb.cnchost.com/nwsltr69.html

36. The Twin Towers Demolition (various slides and notes)

Jim Hoffman

http://911research.wtc7.net/talks/towers/slides.html

37. World Trade Center Building Performance Study

Federal Emergency Management Agency (FEMA)

May, 2002

http://www.fema.gov/library/wtcstudy.shtm

38. World Trade Center History

David Johnson

http://www.infoplease.com/spot/wtc1.html

39. How the World Trade Center Fell

Sheila Barter, BBC, September 13, 2001

http://news.bbc.co.uk/1/hi/world/americas/1540044.stm

40. Feds Withhold Crucial WTC Evidence

Christopher Bollyn, American Free Press, August 8, 2002

http://www.indymedia.org.uk/en/2002/12/48681.html

Books

41. Painful Questions: An Analysis of the September 11ᵗʰ Attack

Eric Hufschmid,

Endpoint Software

2002

42. 9/11: The Great Illusion

George Humphrey

Common Sense Publications

2003

43. The War on Freedom: The 9/11 Conspiracies

Jim Marrs

ARES Publishing

2003

44. Inside Job: Unmasking the 9/11 Conspiracies

Jim Marrs

Origin Press

2004

45. Awakening From Our Nightmare: The 9/11/01 Crimes in New York City

Don Paul and Jim Hoffman

Irresistible/Revolutionary (I/R)

2004

46. The New Pearl Harbor

David Ray Griffin

Olive Branch Press (Interlink Books)

2004

47. 9-11 Exposed

Victor Thorn

Sisyphus Press

2004

48. The 9/11 Commission Report: Omissions and Distortions

David Ray Griffin

Olive Branch Press (Interlink Books)

2005

AFTERWORD

On November 10, 2005, Brigham Young University Physics Professor Steven E. Jones released a report entitled *Why Indeed Did the WTC Buildings Collapse* which postulated that the Twin Towers were not brought down by damage from the airliners' impact on the morning of September 11, 2001, nor the resulting jet fuel fires; but instead were destroyed through the use of "pre-positioned explosives."

Of course other respected sources have spoken out in opposition to the government's "official" version of events, namely Underwriters Laboratory site manager Kevin Ryan, former Bush cabinet member Morgan Reynolds, University of Minnesota Professor James H. Fetzer, and theologian David Ray Griffin, who has authored over 20 books during his career. All of their contributions have lent a great deal of weight to the findings of independent 9-11 researchers; but with Professor Jones' entrance into this highly volatile arena, we now have unimpeachable data from an unimpeachable source that supports virtually every claim we've made in regard to how the World Trade Center towers were brought to their knees.

Naturally, the release of Professor Jones' report was of great interest to me because I had based the entirety of my book *9-11 on Trial* (released February, 2005) on the premise that a controlled demolition was in fact what had destroyed the WTC towers, and not those factors cited by the federal government and its various agencies. Now a tenured professor from a nationally recognized university was speaking on this exact same subject. The biggest question was: would his results coincide with mine?

To my profound delight, after reading Professor Jones' analysis of the WTC collapse, I discovered that his findings supported every major point in *9-11 on Trial* with little, if any, exception. Such corroboration of data is no small feat, for now the 9-11 truth movement has confirmation from a credentialed scientist within the university system saying that the controlled demolitions of the World Trade Center towers was no longer simply a *theory*, but a provable fact backed by cold hard science.

Subsequently, such a development lends a great deal of weight to *9-11 on Trial*, for this was the first book ever devoted solely to the World Trade Center collapses. Of course other authors have devoted individual chapters to this tragic event, but I threw caution to the wind and decided that the WTC controlled demolitions were the crux issue of 9-11, and if we ever wanted to expose who was ultimately behind this disgraceful deed, this is where we should be focusing our energy (and not on other peripheral matters).

Thus, what follows is a sampling of the findings which Professor Steven E. Jones put forth in his above-mentioned report which parallel that which I proposed in *9-11 on Trial*:

• The asymmetrical impacts and asymmetrical fires of WTC 1 and WTC 2 could not produce the symmetrical collapses we witnessed on the morning of September 11, 2001. Asymmetric damage on different structures cannot produce symmetrical results.

• In regard to The Second Law of Thermodynamics, Jones concurs with the analysis in *9-11 on Trial* that the probability of a "complete and symmetrical collapse due to random fires as in the 'official' theory is small, since asymmetrical failure is so much more likely. On the other hand, the major goal of controlled demolition using explosives is the complete symmetrical collapse of buildings."

• Jones says unequivocally that it is likely that there were pre-planted explosives in all three buildings that were destroyed at Ground Zero.

• Likewise WTC 7, which collapsed at 5:20 pm on the afternoon of 9-11, was not struck by an airliner, nor was it subject to 'raging infernos,' yet it fell into its own footprint as did WTC 1 and WTC 2. Jones states with certainty, as did we, that this building could not have come down the way it did except via controlled demolition.

• No steel building has ever in the history of the world (before or since 9-11) collapsed due to fire. But, Jones writes, "Complete symmetrical collapses have indeed occurred many times before – all of them due to pre-positioned explosives in a procedure called implosion or controlled demolition."

• The hydrocarbon and office fires in WTC 1 and WTC 2 did not produce temperatures significant enough to melt the steel beams, and they certainly didn't generate enough energy to produce the molten remains from the steel beams that had been "partly evaporated." To do so would have required temperatures greater than 5000 degrees Fahrenheit, a feat impossible for mere office and/or jet fuel fires.

• In this same vein, molten metal was found in the WTC sub-basements of all three towers, which was still "red hot" weeks after 9-11.

• The National Institute of Standards and Technology (NIST) admitted that the WTC fires were insufficient to melt the steel beams in those structures.

• Although we were told that there were "raging infernos" inside WTC 1 and WTC 2, Jones corroborates our findings that the jet fuel which escaped from each airliner burned off within the first 2 to 3 minutes.

• Massive steel beams which were ejected hundreds of yards from the towers, plus the complete and utter pulverization of hundreds of thousands of pounds of concrete, provide "further evidence for the use of explosives."

• Numerous eyewitnesses and news agencies on the scene that day recounted hearing multiple explosions at the base of each tower on the morning of 9-11.

• Professor Jones reiterates the words of MIT Professor Thomas Eager, who deduced that the jetliner impacts would have been insufficient to topple each tower.

• In opposition to what the government wants us to believe, the World Trade Center towers were not flimsy structures with sub-standard construction qualities, but were instead extremely strong – with 47 steel core columns and 240 peripheral steel beams.

• Using a simple mathematical equation, we can determine how long it should take a structure to collapse when there is absolutely no resistance whatsoever upon it (i.e. a gravity freefall). This gravity freefall is exactly and precisely how each of the WTC towers fell, therefore an incredible energy source must have eliminated ALL the resistance on every single floor.

• Just seconds prior to the controlled demolition of WTC 2, its "cap" toppled 23 degrees past vertical and hung 65 feet over the edge of the remaining structure. In accordance with Newton's First Law of Motion and the law of preservation of angular momentum, this "cap" should have continued falling over onto the streets of Manhattan unless some other energy source caused the entire structure below it to suddenly collapse. Again, such a scenario is only possible via a controlled demolition.

• The "pancake theory" postulated during the PBS Nova special, *Why the Towers Fell*, was nothing more than an elaborate hoax with absolutely no scientific validity.

• In stark opposition to the "scientific method" which states that for a theory to be accepted as true it has to be <u>repeatable</u>, the government's "official theory" lacks repeatability. The observed collapses can not occur again as a result of the "proposed fire-based mechanisms." On the other hand, we could repeat time and time again controlled demolitions that were virtually identical to those that the entire world saw on the morning of September 11, 2001.

I could continue citing dozens of other examples where Professor Jones' data concurs with mine, but I'll instead provide a quote from Kevin Ryan of Underwriters Laboratory: "The probability that fires and [impact] damage (the "official theory") could cause the Towers complete collapse is less than *one in a trillion.*"

Now please think about these words for a moment. There is less than a one-in-a-trillion chance that the government's explanation of events in regard to the WTC collapses is true. Such a statement is of vital importance, especially when it is corroborated by the scientific analysis of Professor Steven E. Jones (not to mention the contributions of Reynolds, Ryan, Fetzer, Griffin, and dozens of other independent 9-11 researchers).

Therefore, the only conclusion we can arrive at is that the government's "official" theory about how the WTC towers collapsed is nothing more than an elaborate fabrication. In addition, we now have respected, credentialed scientists and academicians providing unimpeachable evidence that fully supports the previous findings of many groundbreaking 9-11 investigators who laid the foundation for future studies. Their invaluable work was what allowed me to compile *9-11 on Trial*; and with the release of BYU Physics Professor Jones' report to confirm my findings, we now know that the premise of this book – that the World Trade Center towers were destroyed via three separate controlled demolitions – is 100% accurate.

Prof. Jones' paper, Why Indeed Did the WTC Buildings Collapse, *is online at www.physics.byu.edu/research/ energy/htm7.html. He has presented highlights on the MSNBC TV network and other television and radio channels.*

As if Fate wrote a footnote to the history of the World Trade Center Collapse, on the night of Feb. 12, 2005, the hottest, longest-burning fire of a steel building ever took place with the conflagration of the 32-story Windsor Hotel in Madrid, Spain.

This fire blazed fiercely for 24 hours, and consumed nearly everything in the building that was not steel, completely gutting it – leaving only an intact steel skeleton, an accusing finger pointing to the official lies of 9/11, and to the plain truth: steel structures do not burn down.

Images during and after the Madrid fire may be viewed online at www.reopen911.org.

ABOUT THE AUTHOR

Victor Thorn is the founder of Sisyphus Press, co-host of WING TV with Lisa Guliani, and the author of *The New World Order Exposed*, *The New World Order Illusion*, *America Before the Fall*, *9-11 Exposed*, and the *WING TV 9-11 Collection* on CD-ROM (with Lisa Guliani). He also co-hosted the Victor Thorn Radio Show from 2002-2003 on the Reality Radio Network.

On March 31, 2006, Victor and Lisa Guliani were among the first 9/11 researchers to break into mainstream talk radio, the Lionel Show on ABC affiliate WWOR, for a three hour interview with call-ins on the topic of the controlled demolition of the WTC.

47th floor, going down. The sudden, apparently unprovoked collapse of WTC 7 is for many 9/11 skeptics the smoking gun *non plus ultra* of 9/11. This tower was never hit by any plane. There *are* no photographs of large fires, but there *are* photos showing only two small ones that the fire department is not bothering to fight – and without a single broken window from the ground to the 47th floor. The FEMA report was obliged to discuss WTC 7, but could draw no conclusions about it.

For the 9/11 commission report, the collapse is no part of the Al Qaeda myth, so it simply did not happen. The corporate media studiously ignore it. Public opinion is effectively manipulated by focusing attention on the drama of the Twin Towers, obfuscating the issues around that incident, and hushing up the unexplainable of Bldg. 7. See text *REDUCTIO AD ABSURDUM:* WTC 7 on **page 241 ff.** and video clips of the smoothly gliding collapse at wtc7.net or www.hugequestions.com. Compare also www.controlled-demolition.com.

More from ProgressivePress.com at Your Local Bookstore